The
Leadership Mindset

Transforming Vision into Reality

By
Alex Sterling

The
Leadership Mindset
Transforming Vision into Reality

Table of Contents

Introduction

L eadership, in its essence, is more an art than a science. It's the act of inspiring, guiding, and, most importantly, empowering others to achieve collective goals. While many think of leadership as a trait you're born with, the truth is it can be cultivated and honed with intentional effort and practice. This book is designed to help you do just that—be it steering a multinational corporation, managing a small team, or even leading a startup from scratch.

So, what makes a good leader in today's world? Is it charisma, strategic thinking, or perhaps the ability to foster a sense of community? Quite frankly, it's all of that and more. Leadership is multifaceted, and the complexity only grows with the increasing challenges of a globalized economy, technological disruptions, and diverse workforces. It requires a well-rounded approach. The days of command-and-control are long gone; modern leadership demands emotional intelligence, adaptability, and a genuine interest in people.

You're reading this book because you're ready to take that next step—to enhance your leadership skills for the betterment of your team, your organization, and yourself. Whether you're a seasoned manager, an aspiring leader, or an entrepreneur, the principles laid out in this book are designed to be both actionable and transformative. Expect to dig deep into areas like crafting a vision, strategic planning, and building effective teams. Each chapter offers a roadmap that will help you become a leader who not only excels but also inspires.

To begin with, let's address the mindset. Leadership isn't just about what you do but how you think. The psychology behind leadership influences every action, decision, and interaction you engage in. From understanding your own motivations to recognizing the traits that make successful leaders, adopting the right mindset is your first step toward impactful leadership. When you grasp that leadership is more about servitude than authority, it changes your approach to dealing with people and problems alike.

Consider this a journey grounding itself in a practical framework. In the following chapters, you will discover tools and techniques backed by research, real-world examples, and personal anecdotes. These aren't mere theoretical musings but actionable steps you can incorporate into your daily routine. However, don't expect a one-size-fits-all solution because effective leadership is uniquely personal. What works for one might not work for another; the key is to absorb the principles and adapt them to your context and style.

Vision is the cornerstone of effective leadership. Without a clear vision, you're merely steering a ship without a compass. A compelling vision not only defines the direction but also unites the team towards a common goal. It drives motivation, provides purpose, and sets the foundation for strategic planning. Once you have your vision, the next task is to communicate it effectively.

In the realm of strategic planning, setting goals and priorities is paramount. It's about aligning your strategy with your vision and ensuring everyone in the team understands their role in achieving it. This requires acute analytical skills, a deep understanding of resources, and an unyielding commitment to execution. The strategies you develop should be agile enough to adapt to changes yet robust enough to provide a stable roadmap for progress.

No leader can succeed alone; hence, understanding how to build and nurture effective teams is another crucial aspect of leadership.

From recruiting the right talent to fostering an environment where collaboration flourishes, your ability to engineer a high-performing team will significantly determine your success. Effective leaders are those who recognize that their team's strengths and weaknesses directly impact organizational outcomes.

However, change is the only constant in today's fast-paced world. Organizations are frequently undergoing transformations—be it due to market demands, technological advancements, or internal restructuring. Leading through these changes requires a resilient mindset and the capability to navigate uncertainty with confidence and empathy. Resilience is not merely bouncing back but thriving amidst change.

As you refine your leadership aptitude, you'll also need to master various decision-making techniques. Whether it's analytical decision-making that relies on data and logic or intuitive decisions based on experience and gut feelings, understanding when and how to apply these techniques can make a significant difference. Remember, the goal is to make informed decisions that align with your vision and strategy.

Moreover, emotional intelligence remains an indispensable asset for any leader. This encompasses self-awareness, self-regulation, empathy, and social skills, all of which play a pivotal role in how you interact with and lead others. An emotionally intelligent leader can manage their own emotions and understand and influence the emotions of their team.

Communication skills are, without a doubt, the backbone of effective leadership. The ability to articulate your vision, provide clear directions, and give constructive feedback will directly affect your leadership efficacy. From speaking publicly to actively listening, mastering these skills will enable you to connect better with your team and stakeholders.

Conflict is inevitable. How you handle it can either make or break your team's dynamics. Identifying the sources of conflict and employing effective conflict management strategies will aid in maintaining a cohesive and productive team environment. A leader who navigates conflict with grace and strategy fosters a culture of trust and collaboration.

Innovation and creativity are no longer optional; they're imperative. Encouraging innovative thinking and managing creative teams are pivotal for staying ahead in a competitive landscape. Leaders must create an environment where ideas can flourish, and risks can be taken without fear of failure.

Ethical leadership forms the bedrock of trust and integrity. Upholding ethical principles and maintaining a high standard of integrity influence not just your reputation but also the long-term success of your organization. Ethical dilemmas are common, and how you tackle them will define your legacy as a leader.

Finally, to know whether you're on the right track, you must measure leadership success. Key Performance Indicators (KPIs) and a commitment to continuous improvement will help you monitor progress and make necessary adjustments. Remember, leadership is a journey, not a destination. Assessing your growth, learning from setbacks, and consistently seeking ways to improve are what will make you a standout leader.

Welcome to this incredible journey. It's time to not just learn about leadership but to live it, to breathe it, and to embed it into your very being. As we delve into the psychological underpinnings, strategic frameworks, and actionable insights, you'll find yourself not just leading from the front but leading with heart and purpose. The chapters ahead will guide, inspire, and challenge you, but in doing so, they will also unlock the exceptional leader you're meant to be.

Chapter 1:
Understanding Leadership Mindset

Transitioning from simply managing tasks to truly leading an organization begins with adopting the right mindset. It's about cultivating a powerful combination of self-awareness, vision, and empathy that compels others to follow you. Exceptional leaders don't just react to circumstances; they proactively shape and influence their environment. They're adaptable, understanding that leadership isn't a one-size-fits-all role but a dynamic process that evolves with time and experience. To unlock your potential, focus on the psychology that drives impactful leadership: embracing vulnerability, leading with courage, and fostering an unshakable commitment to your team's growth and success. This mindset shift isn't just theoretical; it's a practical foundation that will fundamentally change how you inspire and motivate those around you.

The Psychology of Leadership

When we talk about leadership, we often focus on skills, strategies, and actions. But at the core, leadership is deeply ingrained in psychology. Understanding the mental frameworks and emotional intelligence that drive effective leadership is essential for anyone aspiring to lead successfully. Leadership isn't just what you do; it's how you think and who you are at your core.

One of the fundamental aspects of leadership psychology is self-awareness. To lead others effectively, you need to understand your own strengths, weaknesses, motivations, and values. Self-awareness allows leaders to be authentic and relatable, creating genuine connections with their teams. Leaders who understand themselves can better manage their reactions and behaviors in different situations, fostering a stable and trustworthy environment.

Influence is another cornerstone of leadership psychology. Unlike manipulation, which aims at control, influence is about motivating people to willingly align with your vision. This requires a deep understanding of human behavior. Leaders who can empathize with their team members, understanding their fears, aspirations, and motivators, can create an atmosphere where people are inspired to give their best.

Emotional intelligence (EQ) is an integral part of this psychological landscape. High EQ allows leaders to connect emotionally with their teams, recognize their own emotional states, and manage relationships judiciously and empathetically. Daniel Goleman, a leader in EQ research, asserts that emotionally intelligent leaders are more successful because they can navigate complex social interactions and lead with compassion.

A key component of understanding leadership psychology is recognizing the need for a growth mindset. Leaders with a fixed mindset believe that their abilities and intelligence are static. In contrast, those with a growth mindset see challenges as opportunities for development and view failures as learning experiences. Leaders who cultivate a growth mindset within themselves and their teams create a culture of continuous improvement and resilience.

Furthermore, the psychology of leadership involves understanding group dynamics. Effective leaders know how to foster a sense of unity and collaboration within their teams. This includes recognizing different personality types and how they work together, resolving conflicts productively, and promoting a shared sense of purpose.

Understanding these dynamics can significantly enhance team performance and morale.

Another fascinating aspect of leadership psychology is the concept of psychological safety. Leaders who create an environment where team members feel safe to express their ideas, take risks, and admit mistakes without fear of judgment or reprisal can drive innovation and engagement. Google's research into high-performing teams found that psychological safety was the critical factor that set successful teams apart.

Self-regulation is a psychological trait that sets exceptional leaders apart. It's the ability to manage your emotions and behaviors in the face of challenging situations. Leaders who practice self-regulation are more adaptable, as they can stay calm under pressure and respond thoughtfully rather than react impulsively. This steadiness often instills confidence and trust among team members.

Leadership also significantly intersects with the psychology of motivation. Understanding what drives individuals and teams is crucial for inspiring high performance. While financial incentives could be a motivator, intrinsic rewards like personal growth, recognition, and the alignment of tasks with personal values often have a far more lasting impact. Leaders need to tap into these intrinsic motivators to fuel long-term engagement and productivity.

In addition to motivation, resilience is a psychological trait that leaders need to cultivate both in themselves and in their teams. Resilience allows leaders to bounce back from setbacks, maintain a positive outlook, and keep moving forward even in the face of adversity. This not only encourages personal fortitude but also sets a powerful example for others to follow.

Moreover, the psychology of leadership involves the ability to manage stress and develop coping mechanisms. Leaders face immense pressures and are often responsible for significant decisions that impact the entire organization. Effective stress management techniques, such as mindfulness, exercise, and time management strategies, can help maintain mental well-being and performance.

Behavioral psychology teaches us about the power of reinforcement and positive reinforcement in particular. Authentic praise and recognition from a leader can boost team morale and performance. Celebrating small wins and acknowledging effort can create a positive feedback loop, encouraging individuals to continue striving for excellence.

The psychological concept of social proof also plays a critical role in leadership. People tend to look to others to guide their behavior and decisions. Leaders who model the behavior they wish to see in their teams can create a culture where those behaviors are emulated and ingrained. Actions truly speak louder than words, and leading by example can significantly amplify a leader's influence.

Lastly, the psychology of leadership also encompasses vision and foresight. Leaders need to have a clear vision of where they want to take their organization and the foresight to anticipate future challenges and opportunities. This visionary aspect requires not only analytical thinking but also a deep understanding of human nature and how people might respond to different scenarios.

To sum up, the psychology of leadership goes beyond mere actions; it's about understanding the intricate workings of the human mind and mastering the emotional and cognitive skills that drive effective leadership. Authenticity, emotional intelligence, self-awareness, motivation, resilience, and vision are just a few of the psychological elements that leaders must cultivate to guide their teams towards success. Leaders who comprehend and harness these psychological principles will be better equipped to inspire, influence, and lead their organizations to new heights.

Traits of Successful Leaders

The core of any successful leader's mindset is the ability to blend a mix of qualities that truly set them apart. These traits are more than just characteristics; they form the bedrock upon which great leadership is built. When professionals understand and embody these traits, they can foster environments that not only thrive but also inspire and engage their teams.

One of the most pivotal traits is **self-awareness**. Knowing oneself—strengths, weaknesses, and blind spots—enables leaders to operate from a place of authenticity. True leaders can assess their skills and knowledge objectively, making improvements where necessary and leveraging their innate talents to their team's benefit. This form of honest self-assessment creates a foundation of trust and reliability, which is critical in any leadership role.

Another cornerstone is *empathy*. Leadership is about people, and at the heart of effective people management is the ability to understand and share the feelings of others. Empathetic leaders foster strong relationships and build bridges of understanding. This quality not only makes teams feel valued and heard but also significantly reduces conflicts. It creates a culture where individuals feel safe to express their ideas and concerns.

Vision sets leaders apart from managers. While the latter may focus solely on managing tasks and ensuring that day-to-day operations run smoothly, leaders work towards a bigger picture. They have the foresight to anticipate future trends and demands. This visionary aspect doesn't just involve having an idea of where the organization should be heading; it also means being able to communicate that vision compellingly. A clear and shared vision aligns the team, providing purpose and direction.

Courage is another essential trait. The path to leadership is fraught with challenges, uncertainties, and decisions that often require taking a stand, even when it's unpopular or risky. Courageous leaders are not afraid to make bold decisions, to speak up for what is right, and to take calculated risks for the greater good. This trait is often what separates those who make a lasting impact from those who don't.

Equally important is *adaptability*. In a rapidly changing world, leaders must be able to pivot and evolve with new circumstances. Adaptable leaders don't see change as a threat but as an opportunity. They are flexible in their approach, willing to embrace new ideas, and can lead their organizations through transitions smoothly.

Effective leaders possess a high degree of *emotional intelligence* (EI). They have the capability to manage their own emotions, as well as the emotions of others. EI encompasses self-regulation, motivation, and social skills, which are all crucial in navigating the complexities of human interactions within an organization. High emotional intelligence allows leaders to create environments of trust, improve communication, and ensure healthy workplace dynamics.

Decisiveness is vital. The ability to make timely and well-considered decisions is a hallmark of strong leadership. Indecision can paralyze an organization, leading to missed opportunities and stagnation. Successful leaders gather the necessary information, weigh their options, and make choices confidently. They understand that not every decision will be perfect, but they value progress over perfection.

Accountability also plays a crucial role in effective leadership. Holding oneself and others accountable ensures that standards are maintained and goals are met. Leaders who take responsibility for their actions, successes, and failures inspire their teams to do the same. It creates a culture of ownership, where everyone feels responsible for the collective outcome.

An often-overlooked trait is *humility*. Humble leaders recognize that they do not have all the answers and are willing to seek advice, listen to feedback, and learn from others. This humility fosters a culture of continuous learning and improvement. It also makes leaders more approachable, encouraging open communication and collaboration within the team.

Let's not forget **integrity**. Leadership without integrity is not sustainable. Leaders with integrity adhere to ethical principles and lead by example. They are honest, transparent, and fair in their dealings. This builds trust, which is the cornerstone of any successful team or organization.

Additionally, **passion** is infectious. Leaders who are passionate about their work inspire others to share that enthusiasm. Passion drives energy, creativity, and perseverance. It can turn challenges into exciting opportunities and flavors the workplace with a sense of purpose and engagement.

A successful leader also possesses strong **communication skills**. They aren't just skilled in public speaking; they are excellent listeners too. Communication involves both expressing ideas clearly and understanding others' viewpoints. Effective leaders ensure that their message is heard, understood, and embraced by all stakeholders.

Alongside communication, *collaboration* is paramount. The ability to work with others towards a common goal amplifies strength. Leaders who actively foster a culture of collaboration encourage their teams to share ideas, support each other, and work synergistically. This teamwork accelerates innovation and problem-solving.

Lastly, **inspirational leadership** cannot be ignored. While management involves dealing with the mechanical aspects of running an organization, leadership is more about inspiration. Leaders who can inspire their teams evoke a sense of commitment and motivation. They create an environment where individuals strive not just for personal success but for collective achievement.

Incorporating these traits into your leadership style will not happen overnight. It requires continual self-reflection, learning, and adaptation. As you journey through this book, you'll find practical steps and strategies to help you cultivate these traits. Remember, successful leadership is a tapestry woven from multiple threads, each contributing to the overall strength and resilience of the fabric.

In summary, self-awareness, empathy, vision, courage, adaptability, emotional intelligence, decisiveness, accountability, humility, integrity, passion, communication, collaboration, and inspirational leadership are the pillars of successful leadership. These traits are not static; they evolve as you grow and experience the multifaceted world of leadership. Embrace them, nurture them, and you'll find yourself becoming the kind of leader who not only achieves goals but also inspires those around you to reach their full potential.

Chapter 2:
Crafting a Vision

Crafting a vision is not just about setting a direction for your organization; it's about inspiring your team to reach for something greater than themselves. A compelling vision serves as a guiding star, illuminating the path through both triumphs and challenges. It's essential to paint a picture of the future that is vivid and attainable, engaging hearts and minds to work cohesively towards a common goal. To achieve this, you need to get everyone on board, from senior execs to the newest hires, making sure they understand and believe in the vision. Remember, a vision should be bold enough to excite but clear enough to guide daily actions. It's this balance that turns a far-fetched dream into a realistic, shared objective. As you move forward, think about how you will articulate this vision, keep it front and center, and align it with every strategic move you make.

Defining a Clear Vision

Crafting a vision is an essential element in leadership that serves as the powerhouse of any successful organization. A clear vision not only charts the course for the future but also defines the purpose that drives every team member towards a common objective. However, defining a clear vision isn't merely an abstract dream or an idealistic goal. It's a blueprint that links aspiration with action, depicting where you want to go and how you plan to get there.

Understanding the significance of a clear vision starts with acknowledging its role as the foundation of strategic planning. As the saying goes, "Without vision, the people perish." Indeed, a well-articulated vision provides the framework upon which all strategic goals are built. This vision acts as a guiding star, illuminating the path during turbulent times and providing clarity when decisions become murky.

A compelling vision must resonate on both an intellectual and emotional level. It should be logical enough to outline realistic and attainable goals, yet inspiring enough to galvanize the team into cohesive action. Great leaders know that for a vision to be effective, it must not only set ambitious targets but also connect deeply with the values and beliefs of those expected to carry it out.

To define such a vision, you must start with introspective questions: What are the core values of the organization? What do we aspire to become in the next five, ten, or twenty years? What kind of impact do we want to make in our industry or community? By reflecting on these questions, leaders can begin to distill abstract desires into precise, actionable statements.

Creating a vision isn't a solitary exercise. While the leader initially delineates the vision, it's crucial to involve key stakeholders in the process. Engaging team members, board members, and even customers in early conversations can provide diverse perspectives, ensuring the vision is inclusive and comprehensive. Furthermore, this collective brainstorming can uncover hidden opportunities and potential pitfalls, making the vision more robust and resilient.

Once the vision is formed, the next step is to articulate it clearly. Simplicity is key. A vision statement shouldn't be a verbose manifesto. Instead, it should be concise, memorable, and capable of being communicated effortlessly. Think of it as the North Star that people can glance at to recalibrate their focus. For example, Google's original vision was to "organize the world's information and make it universally accessible and useful." Simple, direct, and powerful.

Leaders must also be prepared to revisit and refine the vision periodically. No organization operates in a vacuum, and the external environment can change rapidly. Market trends, technological advancements, and socio-economic factors can all influence the relevance and practicality of your vision. Regularly revisiting the vision ensures it remains aligned with the organization's evolving context and aspirations.

In defining a clear vision, it's equally important to ensure it reflects ethical considerations and social responsibility. A vision grounded in strong ethical principles not only fosters trust but also engenders long-term loyalty from both employees and customers. Establishing a vision that prioritizes integrity and ethical behavior can serve as a powerful differentiator in today's competitive landscape.

But merely having a well-defined vision is not enough. It must be backed by a clear understanding of the steps needed to get there. That's where strategic planning comes into the picture, which will be discussed in the next chapter. For now, your focus should be on meticulously crafting a vision that is unequivocal and inspiring.

Defining a clear vision also includes being adaptable and open to iterative improvements. The business landscape is ever-evolving, and what was once a solid vision might need adjustments as new opportunities and challenges arise. Leaders who remain adaptable and encourage a culture of continuous learning can pivot their vision to stay relevant and ahead of the curve.

To make your vision truly impactful, align it with the individual aspirations of your team. Understanding what drives your team members personally and professionally can create a synergistic environment where the organizational vision and personal goals converge.

This alignment multiplies motivation and fosters a sense of shared purpose.

Implementing a clear vision requires that it be embedded into every facet of the organization. It should influence decisions at all levels, from hiring practices to product development and customer interactions. The integration of vision into daily operations ensures a unified approach and consistent progress towards the ultimate goal.

Moreover, incorporating story-telling techniques when communicating your vision can make it more relatable and memorable. Narratives that showcase real-life examples or hypothetical scenarios provide a vivid picture of what the future could look like. This can make the vision tangible, facilitating a deeper emotional connection and commitment from your team members.

One effective method to crystalize your vision is to create a vision board. This could be a simple collage of images, quotes, and statements that visually represent your future goals and aspirations. Vision boards can be placed in communal areas, acting as constant reminders of what you are collectively working towards.

Lastly, a vision must inspire action. It should be a catalyst that turns passive recognition into proactive initiatives. Leaders must embody the vision they've defined, demonstrating through their actions and decisions that they are committed to this future. By doing so, they set a precedent for their teams to follow.

In conclusion, defining a clear vision is about more than setting a high bar. It's about creating a roadmap that combines intention with aspiration. It's about involving your team and stakeholders so that the vision is comprehensive and inclusive. It's about articulating the vision in a way that is memorable and aligned with core values. And it's about ensuring that the vision is not static but adaptable to the ever-changing business landscape. By doing so, you set the stage for meaningful progress and lasting success.

Communicating Your Vision

So, you've crafted a clear vision that's ambitious, compelling, and aligned with your organization's values and goals. Now, the challenge lies in communicating that vision effectively. Communication is more than just sending out an email or making a grand speech; it's about ensuring that every member of your organization understands, embraces, and works towards this shared future. How you communicate your vision can make or break it.

First and foremost, remember that clarity is key. Your team can't follow a vision they don't understand. Use straightforward, jargon-free language to explain your vision. Be precise about what you're aiming for and why it matters. Your vision should answer the big questions: What is our ultimate goal? Why is it important? How will we achieve it? When people understand the "why," they are more likely to buy into the "what" and the "how."

Your enthusiasm is infectious. When you talk about your vision, let your passion shine through. Authentic excitement generates energy and commitment from others. If you believe in what you're saying, others will too. Use storytelling to make your vision more relatable and inspiring. A narrative that connects the company's past, present, and future helps people see their role in the journey. Share personal anecdotes or examples that illustrate the vision in action.

It's also crucial to make your vision co-owned by inviting contributions and feedback. Leaders who involve their teams in shaping the vision create a sense of ownership and inclusion. This collaborative approach fosters a deeper connection to the vision. Host workshops, brainstorming sessions, or smaller team meetings to brainstorm ideas and gather input. Listen actively, showing that each voice matters. You'll not only refine your vision but also reinforce a culture of mutual respect and engagement.

Consistency cannot be overstated when it comes to communicating your vision. Reiterate your vision regularly and integrate it into all aspects of your organizational communications. Align your vision with your strategic planning processes, team meetings, performance reviews, and even day-to-day conversations. Every decision, big or small, should reflect this vision. Inconsistency creates confusion and dilutes your vision's impact.

Leaders must embody the vision in their actions. Walk the talk. Your behavior and decisions should consistently reflect the vision you communicate. Whether it's how you handle client relationships or make internal decisions, model the commitment and values you expect from your team. People look up to leaders who practice what they preach.

Be transparent about the challenges and milestones along the way. Communicating a vision isn't all about painting a rosy picture. Acknowledge the obstacles you may face and be honest about the effort required to overcome them. Transparency builds trust and credibility. Celebrate wins, both big and small, to demonstrate progress and motivate further effort. Recognition reinforces the legitimacy of your vision and keeps morale high.

Harness the power of diverse communication channels. No single method will reach everyone equally well. Use a mix of channels—emails, intranet updates, social media, video messages, town hall meetings, and one-on-one conversations. Each medium has its own strength and can help reinforce your vision differently. Diverse communication strategies ensure that your message penetrates various levels of the organization effectively.

Encourage feedback loops to ensure your vision is resonating. Regularly solicit feedback on how well the vision is understood and how it's being integrated into everyday work. Use surveys, informal check-ins, and focus groups to gauge the pulse of your organization. Be open to adjusting your communication strategies based on this feedback.

Remember, communicating your vision is a continuous journey, not a one-time event. It's about nurturing an ongoing dialogue and continuously aligning your team's efforts with the organizational goals. Keep refining your message and approach as your organization grows and evolves. Effective communication of your vision fuels the collective drive and perseverance needed to achieve it.

By mastering the art of communicating your vision, you empower your team with a clear, shared purpose that propels them towards success. It's about creating a unified force working towards a common goal, unified in understanding and inspired to act. This is where true leadership shines, guiding your organization towards a future filled with promise and potential.

Chapter 3:
Strategic Planning

Strategic Planning is the cornerstone that supports your vision, anchoring it firmly in reality. It's about charting a clear path forward and setting the sails to catch the winds of opportunity. When you meticulously design a strategy, you're not just plotting a course—you're aligning the entire organization with the overarching vision. Goals and priorities shouldn't be mere ambitions, but attainable milestones that guide every step of the journey. Think of your strategy as a living, breathing entity that adapts and evolves with changing circumstances, always staying true to your core vision. The synergy between a well-crafted strategy and a compelling vision can transform challenges into opportunities and aspirations into achievements. This chapter will empower you to build a strategic framework that's robust, flexible, and deeply aligned with your organizational goals, ensuring you're always moving in the right direction with purpose and clarity.

Setting Goals and Priorities

Setting goals and prioritizing them is the cornerstone of strategic planning. Without clearly defined goals, it's like steering a ship without a compass. Goals give direction, purpose, and a sense of where the organization is headed. Priorities, on the other hand, ensure that resources and efforts are focused on what truly matters. Without them, even well-set goals can be lost in the shuffle of everyday tasks.

First off, let's explore why goals are so critical. Goals are not just lofty ambitions; they're actionable targets that align with your vision. They break down your overarching strategy into measurable, achievable steps. Crafting specific, measurable, achievable, relevant, and time-bound (SMART) goals is essential. These criteria transform abstract ideas into actionable plans, making it easier for teams to understand what's expected and for leaders to measure progress.

Effective goals share several common characteristics. They should be clear and concise, articulated in a way that leaves no room for ambiguity. When goals are transparent, it becomes easier for every member of the team to grasp the direction and rally around the cause. This clarity of purpose fosters unity and collective momentum.

Furthermore, prioritize what truly matters can prevent what's often termed as "mission creep." This occurs when additional tasks or mini-goals start to dilute the focus of the organization. By setting and maintaining priorities, you ensure the team focuses on tasks that drive the highest impact, hence safeguarding against the dilution of effort.

Now, let's talk about creating a framework for setting these priorities. One of the most effective tools is the Eisenhower Matrix, a simple yet powerful tool that categorizes tasks into four quadrants: urgent and important, important but not urgent, urgent but not important, and neither urgent nor important. This helps in visualizing which tasks require immediate attention and which can be delegated or deferred.

Balancing short-term objectives with long-term goals is an art that every leader must master. Short-term goals act as stepping stones to achieving larger, strategic objectives. They keep the momentum going and offer immediate gratification, which can provide a morale boost for the team. Long-term goals, on the other hand, may require a more sustained effort but are critical for the organization's growth and sustainability.

In this journey, it's crucial to maintain flexibility. The business environment is dynamic and often unpredictable. While goals provide direction, the path to achieving them might need adjustments. Being rigid can lead to missing opportunities or exacerbating problems. Flexibility ensures resilience, allowing your organization to pivot when necessary while keeping the ultimate objectives in sight.

Another crucial aspect is to align goals with the core values and mission of the organization. When goals resonate with the organizational culture and values, they become more than just targets; they become a part of the organizational identity. This alignment infuses a sense of purpose and fulfillment among team members, driving higher motivation and commitment levels.

Employee involvement in goal-setting is also paramount. When team members contribute to goal-setting, they take ownership and become more committed to achieving these goals. Their insights can also provide valuable perspectives, making the goals more comprehensive and attainable. Engaging the team in this process not only fosters a collaborative environment but also leverages the collective intelligence of the group.

Once goals are set and priorities defined, it's critical to communicate them effectively. Clear communication ensures that everyone is on the same page. Regular updates and transparent communication channels help in tracking progress and making necessary adjustments. It also creates a feedback loop where continuous improvements can be made.

Measuring progress is integral to this entire process. Key Performance Indicators (KPIs) can be an excellent tool for this purpose. KPIs offer quantifiable measures that can be tracked over time, providing insights into whether the goals are being met. Regularly reviewing these indicators helps in making informed decisions and course corrections if necessary.

In essence, setting goals and priorities is not a one-time activity but an ongoing process. It requires unwavering focus, flexibility, and continuous reevaluation. By adopting a structured approach, honing flexibility, and fostering a collaborative environment, you are well-positioned to drive your organization towards sustained success.

Lastly, remember to celebrate successes, no matter how small. Achievements build momentum and reinforce commitment towards the bigger goals. Recognizing and celebrating milestones creates a positive environment and reinforces a culture of accomplishment.

So as you embark on setting goals and defining priorities, do so with clarity, flexibility, and an empowering mindset. It's the mosaic of these well-crafted goals and finely-tuned priorities that will drive your organization to new heights.

Aligning Strategy with Vision

Aligning strategy with vision is the linchpin that holds the architecture of organizational success together. Imagine you're piecing together a puzzle; each piece represents a tactical move, but it's the vision that shows you the final picture. Without a clear vision, strategy becomes a series of disjointed efforts, akin to wandering aimlessly in a thick fog. When strategically planned actions align seamlessly with a well-defined vision, it creates a sense of purpose and direction, empowering teams to move cohesively towards a common goal.

A compelling vision acts as the North Star for your organization. It's not just a lofty statement on a corporate wall—it's the driving force behind every strategic decision you make. Your vision provides context, making it easier to prioritize initiatives and allocate resources. When your team understands "the why" behind "the what," they're more likely to be committed and motivated. This deep sense of alignment fosters a culture where everyone, from top executives to entry-level employees, knows how their work contributes to the broader mission.

Creating this alignment starts by ensuring that your vision is clear and articulated effectively. A vision should be more than aspirational; it must be actionable. For instance, if your vision is to be the leading provider of eco-friendly products, your strategy should include specific initiatives like product innovation in green technology, marketing campaigns emphasizing sustainability, and partnerships with environmental organizations. By breaking down the vision into actionable strategies, you turn abstract ideas into concrete steps that guide daily operations.

To align strategy with vision, it's crucial to involve key stakeholders in the planning process. This fosters a sense of ownership and ensures diverse perspectives are considered. Leaders must create an environment where team members feel valued and heard. When people contribute to shaping the strategy, they're more likely to be invested in its execution. Open dialogue helps identify potential roadblocks and anticipate changes, making the strategy more resilient and adaptable.

Moreover, setting measurable goals is essential. These goals act as milestones that guide the journey towards your vision. Think of them as signposts along a road, confirming that you're on the right path. Goals must be Specific, Measurable, Achievable, Relevant, and Time-bound (SMART). They provide a framework to evaluate progress and make necessary adjustments. Regularly revisiting these goals within the context of your vision keeps everyone focused and accountable.

Communication is another critical element in aligning strategy with vision. Leaders need to communicate the vision consistently and compellingly, ensuring it's understood at every level of the organization. This isn't a one-time announcement but an ongoing narrative. Use various channels—meetings, newsletters, workshops—to reinforce the vision. Celebrate small wins that align with the vision and use them as case studies to illustrate how strategic actions contribute to larger goals. This continuous reinforcement helps embed the vision into the organizational culture.

In addition to communication, aligning strategy with vision requires regular review and flexibility. The business landscape is dynamic, and rigidity can stifle progress. Periodic strategic reviews allow you to evaluate what's working and what isn't. This doesn't mean changing the vision but adapting strategies to remain aligned with it. Being open to change and fostering a culture that's agile and responsive can turn challenges into opportunities, ensuring long-term success.

To bring it all together, let's consider an example. Suppose your organization's vision is to be a global leader in technological innovation. Your strategy might involve a mix of research and development, strategic partnerships, and market expansion. This strategy should be broken down into detailed action plans with timelines and responsible parties clearly defined. Key performance indicators (KPIs) should be established to monitor progress towards the vision. Regular check-ins and updates ensure that the strategy remains aligned with the overarching vision, and adjustments are made as needed.

Leaders must also embody the vision. Leadership isn't just about setting the direction but inspiring others to follow it. When leaders walk the talk, they set a powerful example. Their actions and decisions should consistently reflect the vision, making it clear to the entire organization that the vision is not just rhetoric but deeply ingrained in the daily operations and long-term planning.

Empathy and emotional intelligence play pivotal roles in this alignment. Understanding the fears, motivations, and aspirations of your team members allows you to align their personal visions with the organizational vision. When employees feel their personal growth is intertwined with the company's success, their commitment strengthens. This emotional alignment, built on trust and mutual respect, turns the vision into a shared quest.

Another important aspect is resource allocation. A vision-aligned strategy requires adequate resources—time, money, personnel, and technology. Leaders must be adept at identifying where to allocate resources to maximize impact. This might mean investing more heavily in areas closely tied to achieving the vision while deprioritizing others. It's about making informed choices that reflect strategic priorities aligned with the vision.

Consider also the role of innovation in aligning strategy with vision. The most visionary organizations aren't afraid to innovate. They understand that to achieve exceptional outcomes, they must think outside the box and take calculated risks. Encourage a culture of creativity where new ideas are welcomed, tested, and refined. This not only helps in staying relevant but also propels the organization closer to realizing its vision.

Inclusion and diversity are equally critical in this alignment. When your strategy leverages diverse perspectives, it becomes richer and more robust. A diverse team brings varied insights, which can drive more innovative and effective strategies. Aligning strategy with vision in a way that truly values inclusion leads to a more cohesive and dynamic organization.

Ultimately, aligning strategy with vision is about coherence and integration. Every project, initiative, and task should resonate with the vision. Review your projects and see if they map back to your vision. If not, it's time to re-evaluate. Are they diverting valuable resources that could be better spent on more aligned initiatives? Streamlining efforts to ensure they all contribute to your vision avoids wasted effort and maximizes impact.

In conclusion, aligning strategy with vision is an ongoing, dynamic process that demands clarity, communication, empathy, adaptability, and resourcefulness. As leaders, the responsibility rests on us to ensure that every tactical decision, every goal, and every action aligns seamlessly with the greater vision. When strategy and vision coexist in perfect harmony, they create a powerful synergy that propels the organization towards its ultimate aspirations, fostering a unified, motivated, and high-performing team.

Chapter 4:
Building Effective Teams

In continuing our journey towards becoming transformational leaders, it's crucial to recognize that no vision, however grand, is achievable in isolation. Building effective teams is at the heart of driving organizational success. A powerful team is more than a collection of talented individuals; it's an interconnected group with shared values, a common purpose, and mutual respect. Start by recruiting and retaining talent that aligns with your vision and values. However, assembling a stellar team is just the beginning. Encourage open communication to foster team collaboration and create a culture where innovation thrives, and individuals feel valued and trusted. Leadership is not about being in charge but about taking care of those in your charge. When you cultivate an environment of trust, empathy, and shared goals, your team will be empowered to achieve extraordinary outcomes together.

Recruiting and Retaining Talent

In the journey to build effective teams, one of the most critical components is recruiting and retaining talent. Hiring the right people and keeping them engaged isn't just about filling positions—it's about crafting and nurturing a thriving ecosystem where top talent can flourish. For managers, aspiring leaders, and entrepreneurs, mastering this aspect often becomes the cornerstone of their leadership success.

Start by understanding the market landscapes you're hiring from. It's crucial to recognize that top talent is always in demand. Knowing what motivates and attracts the best candidates allows you to tailor your approach effectively. This means digging deeper into the candidate experience from the initial application to the final onboarding stages. Create an experience that's engaging and demonstrates your organization's values and culture right from the start.

Begin with a clear and compelling job description. Too often, job descriptions are laden with jargon and broad expectations that do little to inspire or inform potential candidates. Instead, focus on clarity and specificity. Detail not just the responsibilities and required skills, but also what success looks like in the role and how it contributes to the bigger picture. When people understand how their role impacts the organization's mission, it ignites a sense of purpose even before they join.

Effective recruitment is as much about attracting candidates as it is about choosing them. Utilize multiple platforms—social media, professional networks, and industry events—to cast a wide net. This ensures diversity in your talent pool, which in turn fosters innovation and different perspectives within your team. Remember, each platform should authentically reflect your company culture and values.

Once you have candidate applications, the selection process needs to be rigorous yet empathetic. Structured interviews are great for standardizing evaluation but balance them with conversational elements. You want to gauge not just competencies but also cultural fit. Behavioral interview questions that explore past experiences and situational questions that offer hypothetical scenarios are excellent in this regard.

Keep the lines of communication open during the entire process. Candidates appreciate timely updates, honest feedback, and transparency. Leaving someone in the dark can reflect poorly on your organization and discourage top talent from pursuing the opportunity further. Remember, the candidate experience doesn't end with the job offer. It's just beginning.

Onboarding is a crucial extension of the recruitment process. It can either solidify a new hire's decision or lead to early departures. Aim for a structured yet flexible onboarding program that encompasses not just the technical training but also cultural assimilation. Introduce them to your organization's history, values, and key team members. Foster an environment where new hires feel welcomed and supported as they navigate their new roles.

Retention begins the moment a new employee starts. People often leave managers, not companies. So, cultivating a healthy managerial relationship is pivotal. Regular one-on-ones, constructive feedback, and a genuine interest in their career development can significantly improve retention rates. Employees need to feel valued, heard, and challenged.

A competitive salary and benefits package is important, but it's not the only piece of the puzzle. Top talent looks for growth opportunities, balance, and a positive work environment. Create pathways for career advancement and ensure employees have access to professional development resources. This could include mentorship programs, training sessions, and educational incentives.

Another cornerstone of retention is fostering a culture of recognition. Acknowledge achievements both big and small. People want to know that their contributions matter. Simple acts of recognition can go a long way in building an emotionally positive workplace. Celebrate team milestones, personal successes, and continuous improvement.

And let's not forget the work-life balance. Burnout is a real threat to employee satisfaction and retention. Encourage flexible work arrangements and actively seek to understand your team's needs. Sometimes, it's about offering remote work options, and other times, it's about recognizing when someone needs a break. An empathetic approach to management will always yield stronger loyalty and engagement.

Employee engagement surveys and regular feedback loops can be instrumental in retaining talent. By consistently gauging the pulse of your team, you can anticipate issues before they balloon into major problems. Act on the feedback you receive and communicate the actions you're taking. This fosters a sense of ownership and collective progress within the team.

Finally, an open-door policy that encourages communication at all levels is essential. When employees feel they can voice their concerns or suggestions without fear, it builds trust. Moreover, it allows you to address challenges promptly and maintain a dynamic, adaptable team.

In conclusion, recruiting and retaining talent is not a singular effort—it's an ongoing commitment. By creating a robust recruitment process, an inviting onboarding experience, and a supportive work environment, you can build a team that not only excels but also stands by you in the long term. Investing in your people is investing in the future success of your organization. Remember, great teams are not just built; they are cultivated with care, empathy, and vision.

Fostering Team Collaboration

Building a high-performing team isn't just about recruiting top talent; it's about creating an environment where team collaboration flourishes. Collaborative teams are like finely tuned orchestras, each member contributing their unique skills while working seamlessly together. To foster this, you must invest in strategies that cultivate openness, trust, and respect among team members.

One foundational aspect of fostering team collaboration is establishing clear communication channels. These channels make it easy for team members to share their ideas, concerns, and updates. Encouraging open dialogue can be facilitated by regular team meetings, digital communication tools, and even informal catch-ups. An environment where everyone feels heard and valued naturally elevates collaboration.

Another crucial element is setting shared goals that resonate with the entire team. When everyone is aligned towards a common objective, it becomes much easier to rally the team and harness individual strengths for collective success. Crafting these goals with input from all team members, rather than funneling them down from the top, ensures higher engagement and commitment.

It's also important to recognize and celebrate diversity within the team. Different perspectives fuel creativity and innovation, making it imperative to encourage team members to bring their unique viewpoints to the table. A culture that respects and values diversity will inevitably see a more dynamic and collaborative team spirit.

However, creating such a culture doesn't happen overnight. It requires intentional and consistent effort from the leadership. Leaders should model collaborative behavior, showing willingness to listen and adapt based on team feedback. They should also create opportunities for team-building activities that reinforce trust and camaraderie among team members.

Feedback is the cornerstone of effective collaboration. Constructive feedback loops enable individuals to understand their roles within the bigger picture, align their efforts, and correct course when needed. Implementing a system where feedback is shared regularly, and not just during annual reviews, can significantly boost team cohesion. It's important for leaders to facilitate both giving and receiving feedback in a way that is respectful and focused on growth.

Technological tools also play a pivotal role in fostering collaboration, especially in today's remote and hybrid work environments. Tools like project management software, cloud-based document sharing, and instant messaging apps can bridge geographical divides and streamline collective efforts. But remember, while technology can facilitate communication, it cannot replace the human element of collaboration. Balancing virtual interactions with face-to-face engagements, whenever possible, is key to maintaining strong team dynamics.

Trust is another crucial factor; it's the glue that holds a collaborative team together. Building trust takes time and consistent positive interactions. Start by being transparent with your team about organizational changes, challenges, and successes. Trust also means empowering your team members to make decisions and take ownership of their projects. When team members feel trusted, they are more likely to collaborate openly and take calculated risks that drive innovation.

One practical way to build trust and promote collaboration is through cross-functional projects. These projects bring together members from different departments to work towards a common goal. Not only do cross-functional teams break down silos, but they also build empathy and understanding across the organization.

Leaders should also be mindful of creating a safe space for team members to express their ideas without fear of judgment. Psychological safety is paramount for fostering collaboration. When team members feel safe, they are more likely to participate actively, share innovative ideas, and take initiative. Creating this environment requires leaders to be empathetic, approachable, and open to feedback themselves.

Encouraging social interactions outside of work can also have a profound impact on team collaboration. Informal gatherings, whether they be virtual happy hours or weekend retreats, help team members build personal connections, which translates into better professional relationships. When people know and like each other on a personal level, they are more likely to work together effectively and support one another.

Mentorship programs within the team can be another powerful tool for fostering collaboration. Pairing new team members with seasoned mentors helps in knowledge transfer, creates bonds, and promotes a culture of continuous learning and support. These relationships can significantly enhance the mentee's integration into the team and their confidence in contributing collaboratively.

It's also critical to address conflicts promptly and constructively. Unresolved conflicts can create barriers to collaboration, leading to a toxic work environment. Leaders need to have the skills to mediate conflicts and guide their teams through resolving issues amicably. This not only restores harmony but also reinforces the message that collaboration and teamwork are prioritized.

In conclusion, fostering team collaboration is a multifaceted endeavor that requires strategic effort, emotional intelligence, and strong leadership. It's about creating a culture that values communication, trust, mutual respect, and continuous learning. When team members feel connected, empowered, and valued, they are more likely to collaborate effectively, driving the organization towards its goals and fostering overall success. By committing to these principles, leaders can cultivate a collaborative environment where teams don't just work together, but thrive together.

Chapter 5:
Leading Through Change

Change is inevitable in any organization, and leading through it requires a unique blend of vision, agility, and empathy. As a leader, you must first embrace change yourself; your team looks to you for cues on how to cope and adapt. This means understanding the emotional landscape of those you lead, recognizing that change can be unsettling, and providing reassurance and clarity. Transformational times are golden opportunities to build deeper trust and loyalty within your team. By cultivating a culture that welcomes innovation and adaptability, leaders can sustain momentum and drive positive outcomes even amidst upheavals. Your role is to act as the anchor while steering the ship through uncharted waters, making tough decisions with confidence and compassion. Nurturing resilience within your team and keeping communication transparent will empower everyone to not just weather the storm but to emerge stronger and more united.

Navigating Organizational Change

Change is the only constant in the world of business, yet it remains one of the hardest aspects for organizations to navigate. Leaders who successfully guide their teams through change not only survive but thrive. So, how do you steer your organization through turbulent times? It starts with understanding that change is not just a process but a journey that requires empathy, decisiveness, and vision.

To begin, let's address the emotional turbulence that often accompanies change. Transformations in organizational structure, culture, or strategy can spark anxiety and resistance. It's vital to acknowledge these emotions rather than dismiss them. Empathy, here, becomes your secret weapon. By understanding your team's concerns, you can better address them. Empathy doesn't mean compromising on your vision; it's about showing that you care and are listening.

Consider change communication as your navigational compass. Transparent and frequent communication can make the difference between smooth sailing and a tumultuous journey. Share the rationale behind the change and the benefits it promises. When people see the bigger picture and their role within it, resistance diminishes. Encourage open dialogue and feedback; make it a two-way street rather than top-down directives.

Uncertainty can breed fear. Therefore, providing clear direction and actionable steps is essential. Lay out what needs to be done, who's responsible, and how progress will be measured. This creates a roadmap for everyone to follow. Ambiguity is an enemy of successful change. Eliminate it by being as clear as possible in your expectations and timelines.

Let's not forget the importance of resilience during change. Both you and your team will face setbacks. How you handle these obstacles will set the tone for everyone else. Demonstrate resilience by remaining steady, optimistic, and adaptable. Share stories of past challenges and how you've overcome them, reinforcing the belief that obstacles are surmountable.

Change often demands new skills and capabilities. Invest in training and development to equip your team for what lies ahead. Provide the resources necessary to adapt, from new tools to educational workshops. When your team feels prepared, their confidence soars, and so does their ability to handle change.

Involving your team in decision-making can foster a sense of ownership and reduce resistance. People are more likely to commit to changes they helped create. Use brainstorming sessions, surveys, and committees to gather input and involve employees at different levels. Empowerment leads to a more engaged and motivated workforce.

You must also be ready to pivot and make adjustments as needed. No plan survives first contact with reality untouched. Monitor progress and be prepared to shift gears based on feedback and results. Flexibility is not a sign of weakness but of a dynamic leadership approach.

It's easy to get lost in the logistics of change, but never forget the human element. Celebrate small wins and milestones to keep morale high. Recognition and appreciation go a long way in maintaining momentum. Throw a mini-celebration when targets are hit, or create informal settings where people can share their successes and challenges.

Amidst all this, your personal growth as a leader is vital. Reflect on your leadership style and adjust it as necessary to meet the demands of change. Are you too rigid? Are you sufficiently empathetic? Continuous self-improvement will ensure you remain an effective leader throughout the transition.

While it's crucial to support your team, don't neglect your well-being. The pressure of guiding an organization through change can be immense. Taking care of your physical and mental health ensures you have the stamina and clarity needed for effective leadership. After all, a burnt-out leader can't inspire or guide a team.

Dealing with resistance is part and parcel of navigating organizational change. Whether it's passive or active, resistance needs to be addressed head-on. Schedule one-on-one meetings to understand individual concerns. Sometimes, simply listening can alleviate much of the pushback.

Team cohesion can be bolstered by shared experiences, including those outside of work. Organize team-building activities to strengthen bonds and create a unified front. A well-connected team supports each other better through transitions.

Let's delve into maintaining the new normal once the initial change has been implemented. Change isn't a one-off event but an ongoing process. Keep the momentum going by continually reinforcing the new behaviors and practices. This ensures that the change becomes embedded in your organization's culture.

Document lessons learned during the transition. What worked well? What could have been better? This repository of knowledge becomes invaluable for future change initiatives and sets a precedent for continuous improvement.

To round things off, let's talk about legacy. Successful navigation through change sets you up as a leader who can be trusted to guide the organization through future challenges. The experiences and lessons learned during this time will shape not only your leadership journey but also the careers of those you lead.

The mark of a transformative leader lies not just in navigating change but in making it a stepping stone for greater organizational and personal growth. Embrace the journey with a steadfast heart and clear mind, and you'll find that change is not just an obstacle, but an opportunity for unparalleled growth and innovation.

And there you have it, the essentials for navigating organizational change. Apply these principles with a blend of empathy, resilience, and clear communication, and you will lead your team not just through the storm but towards a brighter, more promising horizon.

Developing Resilience

Resilience isn't just about bouncing back; it's about bouncing forward. When you're leading through change, developing resilience is crucial. It's your ability to recover quickly from setbacks, adapt well to change, and keep going in the face of adversity. This isn't just about survival; it's about thriving. Let's delve into how you can cultivate this essential quality.

In the landscape of leadership, setbacks and challenges are inevitable. You're going to face tough situations that may test your limits. What's important is not how many times you fall, but how many times you get back up. Developing resilience involves mental toughness, but equally essential is emotional flexibility. Embrace change with an open mind. Understand that each challenge carries with it an opportunity to grow.

Research has shown that resilient leaders not only bounce back from challenges but often emerge stronger. They don't view obstacles as the end. Instead, they see them as stepping stones. One of the most powerful ways to build resilience is by staying connected with your "why." Your purpose. It's the internal drive that keeps you going when the going gets tough.**Self-awareness** is another cornerstone of resilience. Knowing your strengths, weaknesses, and emotional triggers helps you navigate through turbulent times with grace. Being self-aware allows you to understand when you're feeling overwhelmed and take appropriate action. Whether that means asking for support, taking a break, or reevaluating your approach, understanding yourself deeply can make a significant difference.

First, it's essential to cultivate a positive mindset.

Adopt a growth mindset; it's the belief that your abilities can be developed through dedication and hard work.

Acknowledge your vulnerabilities and limitations, and don't be afraid of failure.

Growth mindset pioneers emphasize that failure is not a flaw but a feature of the learning process. The way you frame your experiences can profoundly impact your resilience. Instead of viewing a setback as a defeat, see it as valuable feedback. What can you learn from it? How can you do better next time?

Connections with others also play a crucial role in developing resilience. Build a network of supportive relationships, both personal and professional. These relationships provide emotional sustenance and perspective when you need it most. Don't shy away from leaning on your support system. Engage in open communication, share your challenges, and seek advice and encouragement.

Additionally, practicing mindfulness can significantly bolster your resilience. Mindfulness techniques, such as meditation, deep breathing exercises, and journaling, can help reduce stress, enhance emotional regulation, and improve focus. These practices create a mental buffer against the pressures of leadership, enabling you to respond to challenges with greater clarity and composure.

Another key element in developing resilience is maintaining physical well-being. Physical health directly influences mental and emotional resilience. Exercise regularly, eat a balanced diet, and prioritize sleep. These basic but often neglected aspects of self-care can help you maintain the stamina needed to navigate long-term challenges.

Develop a habit of self-reflection. Take time to pause and assess your journey. What have you learned from your experiences? How have you grown? Reflecting on your progress reinforces your sense of achievement and prepares you for future challenges. It's through such introspective practices that you realize how far you've come and recognize your capacity to overcome obstacles.

One practical approach to building resilience is through setting realistic, achievable goals. Break down larger challenges into smaller, manageable tasks. Achieving these tasks creates a sense of accomplishment, boosting your confidence and resilience to tackle bigger issues.

Resilient leaders also practice adaptability. Change is inevitable, and the ability to pivot when necessary is a hallmark of resilient leadership. Stay flexible and open to new ideas and approaches. Adaptability allows you to navigate through uncertainties and capitalize on new opportunities that arise.

Moreover, fostering a resilient organizational culture can amplify your efforts. Encourage a culture where learning from failure is embraced, and setbacks are viewed as opportunities for growth. Create an environment where team members feel safe to take risks, express their ideas, and learn from their experiences. This collective resilience can make your organization more robust and innovative.

It's essential to lead by example. Show your team how to handle stress and setbacks with grace and poise. Your resilience will inspire and empower others to develop their own resilience. Share your experiences and lessons learned, demonstrating that resilience is an ongoing journey, not a destination.

Lastly, remember that resilience is not about going it alone. Effective leaders know when to seek help and when to delegate. Recognize that resilience includes the humility to acknowledge that you don't have all the answers. Surround yourself with a diverse team, each bringing their unique strengths to the table. Embrace collabo-ration and collective problem-solving.

To summarize, developing resilience involves a multifaceted approach. It's about cultivating a positive mindset, leveraging self-awareness, building supportive relationships, practicing mindfulness, maintaining physical well-being, and fostering a resilient organizational culture. Embrace your journey with an open heart and mind, viewing each challenge as an opportunity to grow. Resilient leadership not only empowers you but also inspires and uplifts those around you.

Chapter 6:
Decision-Making Techniques

Imagine you're at a crossroads where the pressure to make quick, yet impactful decisions is immense, and the stakes are high. This chapter is your guide through that very maze, offering you decision-making techniques that blend analytical rigor with the intuition of seasoned leaders. By harnessing both our rational minds and our gut feelings, we align our choices with our vision and values. We'll explore frameworks that provide structure to our thought processes, helping us to see beyond the immediate and into the strategic. The goal is to empower you to make decisions that not only solve problems but also propel your organization toward success. Whether you're faced with daily operational choices or transformative strategic dilemmas, learning how to leverage these techniques will set you apart as a decisive and forward-thinking leader. Dive into this chapter with an open mind, ready to embrace a balanced approach to decision-making that is both methodical and inspired.

Analytical vs. Intuitive Decisions

In the landscape of leadership, decision-making isn't just a skill; it's a dance between the precise and the perceptive. Both analytical and intuitive decisions play crucial roles, and understanding how to leverage each effectively can profoundly impact your organization's trajectory. It's not about choosing one over the other, but rather knowing when to employ each type for maximum benefit.

Analytical decision-making involves a methodical, systematic approach that relies heavily on data, evidence, and structured processes. Think of it as painting by numbers - it's detailed, objective, and clear-cut. You gather information, analyze the facts, weigh the pros and cons, and arrive at a conclusion. This approach minimizes risks and biases by grounding decisions in reality and empirical evidence.

In contrast, **intuitive decision-making** is like abstract art. It taps into your inner feelings, instincts, and gut reactions. It's less about tangible data and more about your experiences, expertise, and subconscious cues. This style leverages the knowledge you've garnered over years, allowing you to make swift decisions even when confronted with ambiguous or incomplete information.

The beauty of intuitive decision-making lies in its speed and adaptability. When time is of the essence, or when faced with a novel situation where data might be scarce, intuition can guide you to make effective choices. However, relying solely on intuition can be hazardous. It's susceptible to cognitive biases and may overlook critical data points.

Leadership demands a balance. There will be moments when delving deep into data analytics is imperative. For instance, crafting a long-term business strategy or making significant financial investments necessitates a thorough, evidence-based approach. By contrast, in rapidly evolving scenarios like crisis management, effective leaders often need to trust their gut instincts to steer their teams swiftly and decisively.

How do you strike this balance? It's about cultivating self-awareness and understanding your decision-making tendencies. Leaders must recognize their biases, strengths, and areas for improvement. Consider taking time to reflect on past decisions: where did you rely on analysis, and when did intuition guide you? What were the outcomes? Such introspection can provide valuable insights into your natural inclinations and areas that might need a more balanced approach.

One effective strategy is to combine both methodologies. Start with an analytical approach to gather data and understand the landscape. Then, allow room for your intuition to synthesize that information and provide nuanced insights. It's akin to blending the precision of a well-researched report with the storytelling prowess of a seasoned orator. By integrating both, you're not only making informed decisions but also adding a level of depth and foresight that purely analytical methods might miss.

Moreover, value the input of your team. Encouraging a culture where both data-fueled insights and intuitive hunches are respected can enrich the decision-making process. An analytical team member might highlight risks and opportunities through data patterns, while another's intuition could signal underlying issues that data alone doesn't reveal.

In the realm of entrepreneurship, where innovation and agility are key, there's often a higher reliance on intuition. Visionary leaders frequently talk about 'seeing' market trends before they become evident in the data. However, even those gut feelings are grounded in a deep, almost subconscious understanding of their industry, competitors, and customers. It's not magic – it's expertise meeting intuition.

Consider Steve Jobs' approach at Apple. Legendary for his intuitive decisions, Jobs often knew what consumers wanted before they did. But this intuition wasn't arbitrary. It was based on extensive experience, insights into technology trends, and an unparalleled sense of design and user experience. His decisions, though 'intuitive,' were informed by years of immersion in his field.

On the flip side, leaders in industries like finance or healthcare, where precision and risk mitigation are critical, might lean heavier into analytical techniques. Regulatory compliance, patient safety, and financial stability all necessitate rigorous analysis and methodical planning. In these fields, an unchecked intuitive decision could lead to significant repercussions.

Nonetheless, leaders should never ignore the human element of their decisions. Employees' morale, customer satisfaction, and cultural factors often aren't fully captured in data spreadsheets. Here's where intuition complements analysis. An experienced leader can 'sense' a brewing issue among the ranks, perceive shifts in employee engagement, or foresee customer dissatisfaction through subtle cues that data might miss.

Remember, being a skillful decision-maker isn't about always being right; it's about being adaptive and learning from each outcome. When an analytical decision doesn't pan out, reflect and gather insights. What data points were missed? Were assumptions flawed? Conversely, if an intuitive call leads to success, analyze why. Was it purely instinct, or was there hidden data your brain processed subconsciously?

As you navigate your leadership journey, equipping yourself with both analytical tools and honing your intuition will serve you well. Attend workshops, read extensively, and engage in continuous learning to sharpen both sides of the decision-making coin. Practice conscious reflection and seek feedback to understand the impacts of your decisions thoroughly.

In essence, the art of leadership lies in the fluid dance between head and heart. Like a seasoned conductor, you need both the sheet music (data) and the passion (intuition) to lead your orchestra to a harmonious performance. By mastering this balance, you'll not only enhance your decision-making prowess but also drive your organization toward sustained success and innovation.

Decision-Making Frameworks

Navigating the complexities of decision-making in a managerial role can feel like traversing a labyrinth without a map. Yet, having a well-defined framework can transform this convoluted process into a series of systematic, informed steps. Decision-making frameworks serve as the backbone of effective leadership, guiding leaders through uncertainty and turning challenges into opportunities.

One popular and effective framework is the **Rational Decision-Making Model**. This model offers a methodical approach, breaking down decisions into clearly defined steps: identifying the problem, gathering information, evaluating alternatives, making the decision, implementing it, and finally, monitoring the outcome. This systematic methodology not only clarifies each phase but also provides a way to assess the effectiveness of the decision afterward. It's a powerful tool in complex scenarios where weighing multiple variables is necessary.

In today's rapidly changing environment, however, a purely rational approach might sometimes fall short. Enter the **OODA Loop (Observe-Orient-Decide-Act)**. Originally developed by military strategist John Boyd, this framework emphasizes the speed and flexibility needed in dynamic situations. By constantly cycling through the steps of observing the environment, orienting to the new data, deciding on a course of action, and acting, leaders can remain agile. This iterative process allows for rapid adaptation, particularly useful in crisis management or fast-paced business sectors.

Another essential framework is **SWOT Analysis (Strengths, Weaknesses, Opportunities, Threats)**. This approach provides a 360-degree view of both internal and external factors that might impact the decision. By evaluating strengths and weaknesses within the organization and opportunities and threats in the marketplace, leaders can make balanced decisions that leverage strengths while mitigating risks. This holistic perspective encourages a comprehensive analysis, aligning decisions with long-term strategic goals.

Switching gears to more personal leadership styles, the **DECIDE model** exemplifies a comprehensive framework specifically designed for healthcare but adaptable to various industries. It breaks decision-making into six distinct steps: Define the problem, Establish criteria, Consider all alternatives, Identify the best alternative, Develop a plan, and Evaluate the solution. By defining each step, it promotes careful consideration and thoroughness—vital in fields where decisions can have significant consequences.

For those in creative or innovative sectors, the **6 Thinking Hats** framework pioneered by Edward de Bono offers a unique approach. This method involves looking at a decision from six distinct perspectives, each represented by a different "hat": Information (White), Emotions (Red), Judgement (Black), Optimism (Yellow), Creativity (Green), and Process (Blue). This structured yet flexible approach encourages diverse viewpoints, fostering comprehensive and well-rounded decision-making.

In a world driven by data, the **Data-Driven Decision Making (DDDM)** framework stands out as invaluable. This framework emphasizes the collection and analysis of data to inform decisions. By leveraging big data and analytics, leaders can make evidence-based decisions that reduce uncertainty and improve confidence. However, it's critical to remember that data should inform, not dictate, decisions. The human intuition and experience still play a crucial role, particularly when data might be incomplete or ambiguous.

For a more collaborative decision-making process involving multiple stakeholders, the **RAPID framework (Recommend, Agree, Perform, Input, and Decide)** developed by Bain & Company is particularly effective. This framework delineates roles and responsebilities, ensuring clarity and accountability. It's not just about making a decision, but about ensuring that everyone knows who is responsible for each aspect of the process, from initial recommendation to the final decision and implementation.

Blending decision-making frameworks might seem complex, but consider the **Integrated Decision-Making Model**. This model synergizes elements from various frameworks to create a customized approach. For instance, combining the Rational Decision-Making Model's systematic steps with the OODA Loop's flexibility can provide both structure and agility. The importance of integrating frameworks is in their ability to tailor decision-making processes to fit specific organizational contexts and dynamics.

Understanding the psychological aspects that influence decisionmaking is also vital. The **Prospect Theory**, for example, delves into how people perceive gains and losses. Developed by Daniel Kahneman and Amos Tversky, it explains why potential losses often loom larger than equivalent gains, influencing decisions in risk-averse or riskseeking directions. Leaders attuned to these biases can better navigate the emotional and psychological facets of decision-making, fostering more balanced and rational outcomes.

To wrap up, decision-making frameworks are indispensable in guiding leaders through the labyrinth of organizational challenges. They offer structured, repeatable processes that not only enhance decision quality but also boost confidence and accountability. By employing these frameworks, leaders can break down complex decisions into manageable steps, ensuring that they consider all relevant factors and perspectives.

One must remember, frameworks are tools, not rules. They are there to guide you, not constrain you. Use them flexibly and adapt them as needed to fit your unique situations. Whether you are facing a strategic decision, a tactical challenge, or a crisis, these frameworks will equip you with the clarity and confidence needed to lead your organization toward success.

Chapter 7:
Emotional Intelligence in Leadership

Emotional intelligence, or EQ, isn't just a buzzword—it's a crucial element that separates great leaders from merely good ones. To harness the power of EQ, leaders must first cultivate self-awareness and self-regulation, mastering their own emotions to respond rather than react. Empathy and strong social skills are just as vital; these attributes enable leaders to build authentic connections, foster trust, and surge through challenging situations alongside their team. With high EQ, leaders can navigate complexities, drive engagement, and create a workplace culture where everyone feels valued and understood. This chapter dives deep into these dimensions, offering practical insights and actionable strategies to elevate your leadership through emotional intelligence.

Self-Awareness and Self-Regulation

At the core of emotional intelligence is self-awareness. It serves as the foundation upon which all other aspects of emotional intelligence are built. As leaders, recognizing our own emotions and understanding their impact on our thoughts and behavior is essential. Self-awareness allows us to identify our strengths and weaknesses, paving the way for personal and professional growth.

Consider a captain navigating through turbulent waters. If they're unaware of how their anxiety or overconfidence affects their ability to steer, they're more likely to capsize. The same holds true for leaders in an organizational context. Self-awareness acts as a compass, guiding us through complex challenges and ensuring that our responses are appropriate and effective.

However, self-awareness isn't just about identifying emotions; it's also about understanding the triggers behind them. By delving deeper, we can uncover the root causes of our feelings and reactions. This deeper introspection can reveal patterns—perhaps certain situations or individuals consistently stir up frustration or anxiety. Recognizing these patterns enables us to prepare, adapt, and respond in ways that promote positive outcomes.

Imagine you're preparing for a major presentation, and you feel a wave of nervousness. Instead of letting it derail your focus, you acknowledge the emotion and remind yourself of past successes. This kind of self-awareness doesn't neutralize emotions but helps to manage them better.

Leading with self-awareness also means being in tune with how others perceive you. Feedback, whether from peers, subordinates, or mentors, is a valuable tool for gaining perspective. Are you seen as approachable? Too dictatorial? This external perspective can illuminate blind spots, offering a fuller picture of yourself as a leader.

Closely tied to self-awareness is self-regulation, the ability to control or redirect disruptive emotions and impulses. Effective self-regulation starts with a pause—a brief moment to collect your thoughts before reacting. It's about maintaining control in chaotic situations and avoiding rash decisions that could lead to negative consequences.

Take, for example, a heated team meeting. A sudden outburst of anger might alienate team members and disrupt collaboration. Practicing self-regulation, on the other hand, allows you to remain calm, address the issue constructively, and guide the conversation toward a solution.

Self-regulation involves a commitment to honesty and integrity. Leaders who practice self-regulation are transparent about their feelings but choose their words and actions carefully. They demonstrate consistency, which fosters trust and respect among team members. It's not about suppressing emotions but channeling them in ways that are productive and aligned with the organization's goals.

Moreover, self-regulation helps in mitigating stress and avoiding burnout. It encourages a balanced approach to high-pressure situateions. When stress levels rise, those who can regulate their emotions are better equipped to handle challenges without becoming overwhelmed.

Consider the analogy of a thermostat. Just as a thermostat regulates the temperature within a set range to create a comfortable environment, self-regulating leaders strive to maintain equilibrium in their emotional responses. This helps create a stable and positive organizational climate where team members feel secure and motivated.

The benefits of practicing self-regulation extend beyond individual well-being to influence the entire team. Leaders who model self-regulation inspire their teams to adopt similar practices, resulting in a more harmonious and productive workplace. It sets a standard of emotional maturity and resilience that others aspire to emulate.

Developing self-awareness and self-regulation is an ongoing journey. One useful strategy is to engage in regular reflection. Taking time at the end of each day or week to assess what went well, what didn't, and how your emotions played a role can offer valuable insights. This practice can highlight areas for improvement and reinforce positive behaviors.

Mindfulness and meditation can be powerful tools in this journey. By fostering a present-focused mindset, these practices help reduce stress and enhance emotional control. Even a few minutes of mindfulness each day can lead to significant improvements in self-awareness and self-regulation.

Another effective approach is seeking feedback from trusted colleagues and mentors. They can provide candid assessments of how you handle emotions and offer suggestions for improvement. Embracing this feedback with an open mind fosters growth and strengthens your leadership capabilities.

Investing in these practices not only enhances your leadership skills but also positively impacts the people you lead. A self-aware and self-regulating leader cultivates a culture of emotional intelligence within their team, promoting collaboration, innovation, and mutual respect.

Remember, the journey toward heightened self-awareness and self-regulation is not a destination but a continuous process. Each step forward, no matter how small, contributes to becoming a more effective, empathetic, and resilient leader. Embrace the journey with patience and dedication, knowing that the effort you put into developing these skills will yield lasting rewards for yourself and your organization.

In conclusion, self-awareness and self-regulation are not just beneficial—they're indispensable for leaders aiming to drive organizational success. They are the bedrock upon which effective leadership is built, enabling leaders to navigate challenges, inspire their teams, and create environments where everyone can thrive. Investing in these aspects of emotional intelligence sets the stage for a leadership style that is not only effective but also deeply human.

Empathy and Social Skills

Empathy and social skills form the backbone of emotional intelligence in leadership. They're the invisible threads that tie a leader to their team, weaving together trust, understanding, and mutual respect. At its core, empathy is the ability to understand and share the feelings of another person. It's not just about feeling sorry for someone; it's about putting yourself in their shoes and seeing the world from their perspective.

Empathy allows leaders to connect with their team on a deeper level. When employees feel understood and valued, their engagement and productivity soar. Empathy fosters a supportive work environment where individuals feel comfortable sharing their ideas, concerns, and aspirations. This level of openness breeds innovation and fosters loyalty.

Picture a leader who truly listens to their team members, acknowledges their emotions, and responds with genuine concern. This leader creates a culture of trust and psychological safety, making their team more willing to collaborate and take risks. In contrast, a leader who lacks empathy may struggle to build meaningful connections, leading to a disengaged and unmotivated workforce.

Building empathy starts with active listening. It means giving your full attention to the speaker, resisting the urge to interrupt, and providing feedback that shows you understand their point of view. Simple phrases like "I understand" or "That must be challenging" can go a long way in validating someone's feelings. It's also important to be fully present in these conversations, removing distractions and focusing on the person speaking.

Social skills encompass a range of relational abilities that enhance a leader's capacity to interact effectively with others. These skills include communication, conflict resolution, and the ability to build and maintain relationships. In leadership, social skills are about more than just being friendly; it's about influencing and inspiring others, building strong networks, and navigating social complexities with grace.

Effective communication is at the heart of strong social skills. It's not just about what you say but how you say it. Leaders with strong social skills are adept at adjusting their communication style to suit different contexts and individuals. They recognize that an approach that works in one situation may not be effective in another. Flexibility and adaptability in communication are key.

Conflict resolution is another critical aspect of social skills. Conflicts are inevitable in any organization, but leaders who can manage disagreements constructively can turn potential disruptions into opportunities for growth. This requires a combination of assertiveness and diplomacy, ensuring all parties feel heard and respected while moving towards a resolution.

Relationship-building is a long-term investment that pays dividends through a cohesive and supportive work culture. Strong relationships are built on trust, mutual respect, and shared goals. Leaders should foster connections not only within their teams but across the organization. Networking and relationship-building shouldn't be confined to formal settings; informal interactions can often pave the way for deeper connections.

Empathy and social skills also play a crucial role in leadership authenticity. Leaders who are empathetic and socially skilled come across as more genuine and relatable. Authenticity breeds trust, and when people trust their leaders, they're more likely to be engaged and committed. Authentic leaders are transparent, admit their mistakes, and show vulnerability, making them more approachable and human.

Developing empathy and social skills is not a one-time effort but a continuous process. It requires self-reflection, feedback, and a willingness to grow. Leaders can benefit from seeking feedback from their team members, mentors, or coaches to identify areas for improvement. Regular self-assessment helps leaders stay aware of their emotional impact and adjust their approach as needed.

Technology can be a double-edged sword when it comes to empathy and social skills. While it provides tools for communication and collaboration, it can also create barriers to genuine connection. Leaders need to be mindful of how they use technology, ensuring it enhances rather than hinders interpersonal interactions. Virtual meetings, for example, can be enriched with techniques that foster engagement and connection, such as turning on cameras and actively involving participants.

Empathy and social skills are not just essential for day-to-day interactions but also for navigating times of crisis or change. During such times, the emotional well-being of team members is put to the test, and empathetic leadership can make a significant difference. Leaders who can sense the emotional climate and respond accordingly can help their teams navigate challenges with resilience and cohesion.

In summary, empathy and social skills are foundational elements of emotional intelligence that every leader should cultivate. They are the keys to building strong, trusting relationships, leading with authenticity, and creating a positive and productive organizational culture. By making a conscious effort to develop these skills, leaders can enhance their effectiveness and drive their teams toward success. Remember, great leadership starts with understanding and connecting with people on a human level.

Chapter 8:
Communication Skills

Communication skills lie at the heart of effective leadership, serving as the bridge between vision and execution. To inspire, guide, and influence, leaders must excel in both public speaking and active listening. Public speaking isn't just about delivering eloquent speeches; it's about connecting with your audience, sharing your vision authentically, and instilling confidence. Likewise, active listening goes beyond nodding along; it's about truly understanding your team's perspectives, asking insightful questions, and providing meaningful feedback. When leaders communicate effectively, they foster a culture of transparency and trust, empowering their teams to achieve greater heights. Remember, the essence of powerful communication in leadership is not just to be heard but to be understood and to inspire action.

Effective Public Speaking

Effective public speaking is much more than just standing in front of an audience and delivering a speech. It's about connecting, engaging, and inspiring. For anyone aspiring to a leadership role or looking to enhance their capacity to influence others, mastering the art of public speaking is crucial. Leaders must convey their vision in compelling ways that resonate deeply with their teams, stakeholders, and larger audiences.

Think about it for a moment: when you remember some of the world's most impactful leaders, what often comes to mind first? Speeches that moved millions, moments of oratory that sparked change, words that rallied support or instilled confidence. This is the power of effective public speaking. It's as much about authentic delivery as it is about the meticulously chosen message.

First, consider the *preparation*. Effective public speaking begins long before you stand at the podium. It's essential to know your audience. Are they industry professionals, team members, potential investors, or the general public? Understanding the demographic will help you shape your message to meet their interests and expectations. Create relatable content that resonates with their experiences, challenges, and aspirations.

Craft a clear and coherent message. Your speech should have a logical flow, starting with an engaging introduction, followed by your main points, and concluding with a powerful closing statement. Use stories, anecdotes, and metaphors to illustrate your points. These elements can make your message more memorable and relatable. Don't overload your speech with data; instead, choose a few compelling statistics that underline your core message. Balance logic with emotion.

Rehearsal is just as important. Practice your speech multiple times, but don't memorize it word for word. The goal is to be familiar enough with your material that you can speak confidently and adapt if necessary. Record yourself, listen to your intonation, pitch, and pace. Maintain a conversational tone to remain approachable and engaging.

Your *body language* plays a significant role in how your audience perceives you. Standing tall, making eye contact, and using hand gestures can enhance your message and make you appear more confident. Conversely, crossing your arms, slouching, or avoiding eye contact can make you seem disinterested or untrustworthy.

Remember, your body should complement your words, reinforcing your message through non-verbal cues.

Consider incorporating the power of *pause*. Silence isn't just the absence of sound; it's a powerful tool that can add weight to your words. A well-timed pause can emphasize a point, give your audience time to reflect on a significant statement, or build anticipation for what comes next.

Engage your audience. Public speaking isn't a one-way street; it's a dialogue. Ask rhetorical questions, incorporate humor where appropriate, and invite interaction. Acknowledging nods, smiles, or even puzzled looks can help you gauge the audience's reaction and adjust in real-time.

Harness the power of *storytelling*. People are naturally drawn to stories. Our brains are wired to remember narratives far better than abstract concepts or lists of facts. Frame your speech around a personal story, a historical event, or a hypothetical scenario that ties into your message. A well-told story can evoke emotions, foster empathy, and make your message stick.

Handling *nervousness* is another critical aspect. Even the most seasoned speakers can feel a bout of nerves before speaking. The key is to channel that energy positively. Deep breathing exercises, visualization techniques, or even a motivating self-talk can help calm your nerves. Remember that a bit of nervous energy can improve your alertness and keep you focused.

Don't shy away from *authenticity*. Authentic speakers are those who connect with their audience on a genuine level. Share personal insights, admit to past mistakes, or highlight moments of vulnerability. Authenticity fosters trust and credibility. It's okay not to be perfect; audiences appreciate speakers who are genuine, relatable, and human.

The art of *feedback* should not be overlooked. After your speech, seek constructive feedback. Ask trusted colleagues or mentors to critique your performance. Pay attention to areas for improvement, but also acknowledge what you did well. Continuous improvement is key to becoming a more effective public speaker.

As you advance in your public speaking journey, exploring various *speaking styles* can widen your range. Whether it's an informational talk, a motivational speech, or a formal presentation, adapting your style to fit the context and audience will enhance your effectiveness. Each setting may require different techniques, tones, and forms of engagement.

Remember, every great public speaker started somewhere. It's a skill honed over time with practice, feedback, and refinement. Don't be discouraged by initial setbacks or less-than-perfect performances. Each speech is a step forward, a learning opportunity to grow and develop your unique voice.

In conclusion, effective public speaking is an amalgamation of preparation, practice, engagement, and authenticity. It's about conveying your message in a way that not only informs but also inspires action. As leaders, our voice is one of our most powerful tools. Let's use it wisely and passionately to drive our visions forward, influence change, and leave a lasting impact.

Active Listening and Feedback

Active listening and feedback are cornerstones of effective communication. For anyone in a managerial role or aspiring to lead, mastering these skills can significantly enhance your ability to connect with and motivate your team. It's not just about hearing words; it's about understanding the meaning behind them. This depth of understanding fosters a culture of trust and respect, which ultimately drives organizational success.

Active listening involves fully concentrating, understanding, responding, and then remembering what is being said. It's more than just passively hearing the words of the speaker; it requires effort and genuine engagement. When team members feel truly heard, they're more likely to be open, honest, and collaborative. This paves the way for more innovative ideas and effective problem-solving.

One of the key elements of active listening is giving your undivided attention. In our fast-paced world, distractions are everywhere. But when you're in a conversation, whether in person or virtual, it's essential to minimize these distractions. Put your phone on silent, close unnecessary tabs on your computer, and focus on the conversation at hand. This simple act of focus can make a huge difference in the quality of the communication.

Another crucial aspect is showing that you're actively engaged. Nodding, maintaining eye contact, and using affirmative phrases like "I understand," or "That makes sense," can reassure the speaker that you're paying attention. These small gestures can make the speaker feel valued and respected, fostering a deeper connection.

Ask open-ended questions to delve deeper into the topic. This not only shows that you're interested but also helps clarify any ambiguous points. For example, if a team member expresses frustration about a project, you might ask, "Can you tell me more about what specifically is causing this frustration?" Such questions encourage elaboration and provide you with more context to better understand the issue.

Paraphrasing and summarizing are powerful techniques in active listening. By repeating back in your own words what the speaker has said, you confirm your understanding and show that you're truly listening. For instance, you could say, "So what I'm hearing is that the timeline for the project feels too tight, and you're concerned about meeting the deadline without compromising quality. Is that correct?"

This approach can clear up misunderstandings and ensure that you both are on the same page.

Feedback is the natural partner to active listening. Effective feedback is timely, specific, and actionable. It's not just about pointing out what went wrong but also about recognizing what went right. Balanced feedback can motivate your team and drive continuous improvement. When delivered with empathy and a focus on growth, feedback can become a powerful tool for development.

First, let's tackle the timing of feedback. Feedback should be given as close to the event as possible, while the experience is still fresh. Waiting too long can dilute the impact and make it less relevant. However, the environment must also be considered. Ensure the setting is appropriate and private if needed, making the conversation constructive rather than confrontational.

Being specific in your feedback is vital. Vague comments like "Good job" or "You need to improve" don't provide enough context or direction. Instead, detail what was good or what needs improvement. For instance, "Your presentation was engaging and well-structured, especially the part where you outlined the project's next steps. However, I noticed some confusion during the Q&A section. Let's work on anticipating potential questions in the future." This gives both praise and constructive advice tailored to actual observations.

Actionable feedback is also key. It's not enough to tell someone what they did wrong; you need to guide them on how to improve. Practical steps and suggestions can help team members understand what needs to be done differently. For example, "Next time, try to format your reports more clearly by using bullet points and headers—this can make the information easier to digest."

Empathy in feedback can open up a dialogue rather than shutting it down. When feedback is delivered with empathy, it acknowledges the person's feelings and perspectives. Using "I" statements rather than "you" statements can soften the message. For example, instead of saying, "You missed the deadline," you could say, "I noticed the deadline was missed, and I understand that things can sometimes get overwhelming. Let's talk about what happened and how we can prevent this in the future."

Regular feedback, rather than waiting for annual reviews, helps in keeping communication lines open and makes performance management more dynamic. Frequent, informal feedback sessions reinforce learning and improvement consistently, preventing surprises at year-end reviews. This approach builds a culture of continuous growth and mutual trust.

Combining active listening with feedback can create a cycle of continuous improvement. When you actively listen, you're more likely to understand your team members' needs and perspectives. This understanding makes your feedback more relevant and impactful. Conversely, when you give effective feedback, you foster an environment where your team feels heard and valued, reinforcing their willingness to communicate openly.

Leading through active listening and feedback is not just about improving performance. It's about building relationships and trust within your team. When you show that you value their input and are committed to their development, team members are more engaged and motivated. This, in turn, can enhance your leadership effectiveness and drive organizational success.

Active listening and feedback are dynamic, ongoing processes. They require commitment and practice but pay dividends in team cohesion and performance. As you hone these skills, you'll likely notice more openness, more innovative solutions, and a stronger, more resilient team.

In conclusion, by mastering active listening and giving constructive feedback, you're not just providing guidance; you're also learning from your team. This reciprocal process builds a culture of trust and respect, which is essential for any successful organization. Keep practicing these skills and watch as your ability to lead, inspire, and achieve results grows exponentially.

Chapter 9:
Conflict Resolution

In any dynamic, thriving organization, conflict isn't just inevitable—it's a sign that people are engaged, passionate, and committed to their work. Effective leadership is less about avoiding conflict and more about transforming it into a catalyst for innovation and growth. This chapter focuses on identifying sources of conflict and offers practical strategies for managing and resolving these tensions constructively. Keep in mind, successful conflict resolution isn't about winning arguments or imposing decisions; it's about creating an environment where every voice is heard, and every perspective is valued. By leaning into empathy, maintaining open and honest communication, and using structured conflict resolution frameworks, you can turn potential roadblocks into pathways for collective progress. Recognize that conflict, when managed with clarity and respect, can become a powerful tool for strengthening relationships, fostering collaboration, and driving your organization forward.

Identifying Sources of Conflict

In any organization, conflict is an inevitable aspect of human interaction. It's not something that can be completely avoided, but understanding the common sources of conflict can help leaders address these issues more effectively. The key is to identify the root causes early and accurately, which makes it easier to manage and resolve conflicts before they escalate into larger problems.

First and foremost, one of the primary sources of conflict is **communication breakdowns**. Imagine a scenario where team members interpret a project brief differently, leading to misunderstandings and frustration. It's like playing a game of "telephone," where the message gets distorted as it passes along. Clear and consistent communication is crucial, and leaders must ensure that all channels of communication are open and transparent.

Another frequent source of conflict is **resource scarcity**. Whether it's budget constraints, limited manpower, or tight timelines, competing for resources can create friction among team members. Leaders must prioritize resource allocation and find a way to balance the needs of different projects and departments. When resources are scarce, fostering a collaborative environment where team members feel heard and valued can make all the difference.

Differences in values and beliefs often lead to conflict, especially in diverse teams. These differences can be cultural, generational, or based on individual backgrounds and experiences. While diversity brings a wealth of perspectives and ideas, it also requires a leader who can cultivate an inclusive culture and encourage respectful discourse. By promoting empathy and understanding, leaders can harness the power of diversity rather than allowing it to be a source of division.

The next significant source of conflict is **unmet expectations**. Whether it's an employee who feels they deserve a promotion or a team member who expected more support on a project, unfulfilled expectations can lead to dissatisfaction and disengagement. Setting clear expectations from the outset and maintaining regular check-ins can help prevent this type of conflict. Leaders should be proactive in addressing concerns and managing expectations to ensure alignment with organizational goals.

Personality clashes are another common source of conflict in the workplace. Each individual brings their unique personality traits, work styles, and temperaments to the table. While these differences can be an asset, they can also lead to misunderstandings and tension. Leaders play a crucial role in recognizing and mediating these clashes by fostering a work environment that values diversity of thought and encourages collaboration.

A fourth source of conflict includes **role ambiguity and responsibilities**. When employees are unsure of their roles, response-bilities, and expectations, confusion ensues, creating an environment ripe for conflict. It's essential for leaders to provide clarity and ensure that every team member understands their specific duties and how they contribute to the organization's overarching goals. Regular performance reviews and feedback sessions can aid in maintaining this clarity and preventing role-related conflicts.

Power struggles can also lead to conflict, particularly in hierarchical organizations where competition for leadership roles and promotions is fierce. This type of conflict can be damaging as it fosters a "win-lose" mentality rather than a "win-win" mindset. Leaders must create a culture of meritocracy and collaboration where individuals feel their contributions are recognized and valued, regardless of their position in the organizational hierarchy.

The **pressure to perform** and achieve targets can also be a source of conflict, especially in high-stakes environments. Stress and anxiety can amplify disagreements and create a tense atmosphere. Here, emotional intelligence is key. Leaders should be aware of the stressors affecting their team and provide the necessary support to help them manage pressure effectively, including promoting work-life balance and mental health initiatives.

Lastly, unresolved past conflicts can linger and resurface, leading to recurring tension. It's like a wound that hasn't fully healed, susceptible to re-injury. Leaders must address conflicts head-on and work toward comprehensive resolutions rather than allowing issues to fester. This includes fostering an environment where feedback is welcomed and acted upon promptly, allowing team members to move forward with trust and collaboration.

Understanding these sources of conflict helps leaders not only in identifying them early but also in taking preemptive measures to mitigate their impact. By being proactive and cultivating an environment where communication is clear, resources are well-managed, and diversity is celebrated, leaders can turn potential points of conflict into opportunities for growth and innovation. Conflict, when managed effectively, doesn't just resolve issues; it strengthens the overall fabric of the organization, paving the way for success.

Strategies for Conflict Management

Conflict is inevitable, especially in high-stakes environments where decisions need to be made rapidly and unanimously. The key isn't in avoiding conflict, but rather in how we manage and resolve it. Effective conflict management can mean the difference between a high-performing team and a dysfunctional one. Let's delve into some actionable strategies that can transform conflicts into pathways for growth and innovation.

Embrace Open Communication

The first step in managing conflict is ensuring that lines of communication are open. When team members feel heard, they're more likely to engage in problem-solving rather than finger-pointing. Create an environment where everyone feels safe to express their views without fear of retribution. This may include adopting an open-door policy, regular check-ins, or setting up anonymous feedback systems.

Sometimes, it's essential to read between the lines. People may not always vocalize their concerns directly, but non-verbal cues or a dip in productivity can signal underlying issues. As a leader, be proactive in asking questions like, "Is there something more we should discuss?" This shows that you value their input and are committed to finding solutions.

Active listening plays a crucial role. Engage fully with the person talking to you, avoid interrupting, and reflect back what you've heard. This validates their emotions and shows you are genuinely interested in their perspective. For instance, saying, "It sounds like you're frustrated with the current process. Let's explore how we can make it better," reaffirms their concerns and sets the stage for collaborative problem-solving.

Implement Conflict Resolution Frameworks

Having a structured approach to conflict resolution can provide clarity and consistency. Frameworks like the Thomas-Kilmann Conflict Mode Instrument (TKI) can be incredibly useful. TKI identifies five conflict-handling modes:

Competing

Collaborating

Compromising

Avoiding

Accommodating

Understanding these modes can help you choose the best approach based on the situation and the stakes involved. For example, collaborating may be ideal for complex issues requiring multiple viewpoints, while accommodating might be better suited for minor disputes where maintaining harmony is more important.

It's also beneficial to follow a step-by-step process for conflict resolution. One effective method includes:

Identify the problem: Clearly define what the conflict is about.

Understand everyone's interests: Get to the root causes by understanding each party's underlying concerns.

List possible solutions: Brainstorm without judgment to keep creativity flowing.

Evaluate options: Discuss the pros and cons of each solution.

Agree on a solution: Aim for consensus while considering all viewpoints.

Implement and follow-up: Put the agreed solution into action and review its effectiveness over time.

These steps can turn a chaotic conflict into a structured discussion focused on tangible outcomes.

Promote Emotional Intelligence

Leaders with high emotional intelligence (EQ) are more adept at managing conflicts. This involves being self-aware, controlling your emotions, demonstrating empathy, and handling interpersonal relationships judiciously and empathetically. Training your team in EQ can be a game-changer, enabling members to manage their emotions and understand the emotional triggers of others.

Encourage empathy by asking team members to step into each other's shoes. For instance, during a heated discussion, you could say, "Let's take a moment to understand why this issue is important to James," or "Can we get a sense of how Maria's view impacts the project?". Such approaches help to diffuse tension and foster a culture of understanding.

Moreover, self-regulation is vital. As a leader, your ability to stay calm and composed during a conflict sets the tone for the entire team. Techniques such as deep breathing, taking a short break, or even practicing mindfulness can be useful tools to keep your emotions in check during conflict situations.

Leverage Mediation Techniques

Sometimes, conflicts escalate to a level where a neutral third party is essential. In such cases, adopting mediation techniques can help. Mediators guide the conflicting parties toward a mutually acceptable resolution. The key is neutrality; the mediator must facilitate the discussion without taking sides.

Prepare a mediation session by setting ground rules, such as no interrupting and respecting different perspectives. Use phrases like, "I encourage you to express concerns without assigning blame." This encourages a focus on solutions rather than personal attacks. Break the issue into smaller parts if it's overwhelming, addressing one concern at a time.

Mediators should also help conflicting parties understand each other's perspectives. Phrases like, "What I hear you saying is..." can be instrumental in this process. This not only validates emotions but also clarifies misunderstandings that may be fueling the conflict.

Set Clear Expectations and Consequences

Prevention is often better than cure. Setting clear expectations about acceptable behavior and communication can prevent many conflicts from arising in the first place. Establishing a robust code of conduct and ensuring everyone understands the consequences of deviating from it can maintain harmony.

Discuss these expectations openly with your team. For example, you might say, "We're all committed to maintaining a respectful and constructive dialogue, even when we disagree." Reinforce these expectations regularly during team meetings and through one-on-one interactions.

When consequences are necessary, apply them consistently and fairly. If a team member repeatedly disregards group norms, address it privately and constructively. Focus on the impact of their behavior rather than personal attributes. For instance, "I've noticed that interruptions have increased during meetings. This disrupts our flow and prevents us from hearing all perspectives," is a non-judgmental way to address the issue.

Encourage a Collaborative Culture

Ultimately, fostering a collaborative culture can reduce the frequency and intensity of conflicts. Collaboration thrives on mutual respect, shared goals, and a sense of community. As a leader, champion collaboration by recognizing and rewarding behaviors that contribute to a team-first environment.

Create opportunities for team bonding through joint projects, off-site retreats, or even informal get-togethers. These activities build trust and understanding, which can prevent conflicts from taking root. Additionally, highlight examples where collaboration led to success. This can be as simple as saying during a meeting, "Remember how well we came together to tackle the last project? Let's bring that same energy to this challenge."

Encouraging transparency can also foster a collaborative spirit. Share information openly and involve team members in decision-making processes wherever possible. This not only builds trust but also empowers individuals, reducing feelings of disenfranchisement that

Chapter 10:
Innovation and Creativity

Innovation and creativity aren't just buzzwords; they're essential components that drive organizational success. For leaders, fostering an environment where unconventional ideas can thrive means moving beyond traditional boundaries and inspiring teams to explore uncharted territories. It's about cultivating a culture that encourages risk-taking and perceives failures as stepping stones rather than setbacks. To truly unlock the potential within your team, it's vital to establish trust and empower individuals to voice their creative insights. The interplay between encouraging innovative thinking and managing creative teams creates a dynamic ecosystem where groundbreaking solutions can emerge. Remember, the path to innovation often starts with a simple question: "What if?" By blending visionary thinking with a supportive atmosphere, leaders can harness creativity to propel their organizations forward.

Encouraging Innovative Thinking

Achieving a competitive edge in today's fast-paced world hinges on our capability to think innovatively. As leaders, it's our job to cultivate environments where creativity thrives. This isn't just a nice-to-have; it's essential. Encouraging innovative thinking requires a combination of setting the right tone, nurturing talent, and fostering an atmosphere where unconventional ideas are not only welcomed but celebrated.

Firstly, let's talk about the tone and culture you create as a leader. You set the stage. Your team takes cues from you on what's acceptable and what's not. By openly valuing curiosity and questioning the status quo, you let your team know that innovation is a priority. If employees feel safe enough to voice their unorthodox ideas without fear of ridicule, you're already halfway there.

But how do we go about cultivating such an environment? Start with creating opportunities for brainstorming and open dialogue. Make it a habit to hold regular ideation sessions where all contributions are valued equally, regardless of rank or department. During these sessions, encourage wild ideas—they're often the breeding ground for breakthrough innovations.

Innovation isn't just about waiting for that "aha!" moment. It's about a structured approach where creativity is systematically encouraged. Using methods like Design Thinking or the Lean Startup approach can be profoundly effective. These methodologies offer a framework to explore creative solutions and quickly iterate based on feedback. By integrating these into your team's workflow, you not only promote innovation but also create a more dynamic and adaptable organization.

Transforming your team's mindset towards one that embraces innovation isn't an overnight process. It's like nurturing a garden; it takes patience, care, and constant attention. Start by encouraging your team to view challenges as opportunities rather than obstacles. A problem-solving mindset is often the catalyst for innovative thinking. When an issue arises, pose it as a question to the team and encourage everyone to brainstorm potential solutions. Approach setbacks not as failures but as learning experiences.

A crucial component of encouraging innovative thinking is maintaining an environment that celebrates failure as part of the learning process. Thomas Edison famously said, "I have not failed. I've just found 10,000 ways that won't work." This sentiment should resonate within your organization. When failure is punished, people become risk-averse, and creativity stalls. Conversely, when failure is seen as a step toward success, innovation flourishes.

Equipping your team with the right tools can also make a significant difference. Leverage technology to foster collaboration and idea generation. Tools like mind-mapping software, collaborative platforms, and even casual chat applications can facilitate the flow of ideas. Providing resources like access to creativity workshops or ongoing education can also spark new ways of thinking.

Another often overlooked aspect is the physical space in which your team works. Creativity often thrives in environments that break the mold of traditional office settings. Consider incorporating open spaces, zones for quiet contemplation, and areas designed for informal gatherings. Just shifting the physical environment can often unlock fresh perspectives and ideas.

Leadership also involves recognizing and nurturing each individual's unique strengths and passions. Knowing your team members well enough to spot where their creativity lies can be immensely beneficial. Perhaps some of your team excel in visual thinking, while others are great at analytical problem-solving. By harnessing these diverse talents collectively, you can create a symphony of innovative thinking.

Encouraging innovative thinking also requires a commitment to ongoing learning and development. Curiosity fuels innovation, and a curious team is always exploring new possibilities. Encourage your team to engage in continuous learning, whether through formal education, attending industry conferences, or simply reading widely. The cross-pollination of ideas from different fields can often lead to truly groundbreaking innovations.

Leaders should also be open to learning and growing alongside their team. Demonstrating a willingness to adapt and evolve not only sets a strong example but also keeps the leader attuned to emerging trends and fresh ideas. By maintaining a mindset of continuous improvement, leaders can inspire their teams to think innovatively.

Empathy is another powerful tool in fostering innovation. By understanding the needs and desires of your customers or clients, you can guide your team to develop solutions that are not just novel but truly meaningful. Empathy-driven innovation often leads to products and services that resonate deeply with users, creating lasting value.

The power of diversity, too, can't be understated. When teams are composed of individuals with varied backgrounds, experiences, and perspectives, the range of ideas expands exponentially. Encourage hiring practices that prioritize diversity and inclusion. This isn't just about demographic variety but also about cognitive diversity— different ways of thinking, problem-solving, and approaching challenges.

Incentives can also play a role, but they need to be structured carefully. While traditional rewards like bonuses and promotions have their place, consider implementing recognition programs that celebrate creative achievements. Sometimes, simply acknowledging and showcasing innovative work can be a significant motivator.

The process of idea implementation is another vital aspect. It's not enough to just generate ideas; there must be a clear path to execution. Encourage a culture where ideas are not just discussed but also prototyped, tested, and refined. Provide the resources necessary to take an idea from concept to reality, and celebrate each step of the process.

Building a culture of innovation also means being willing to break away from the norm and allowing your team the freedom to explore. Encourage them to take "creative time outs"—periods where they can step away from their routine tasks to focus solely on exploring new ideas. A company might, for example, dedicate one day a month for employees to work on any project they're passionate about, no strings attached. This kind of freedom can yield unexpected and transformative innovations.

Lastly, it's essential to communicate the value of innovation consistently. Speak openly about the importance of creativity in achieving the organization's vision and goals. When team members see that innovation is a priority at the highest levels and is integrated into the strategic objectives, they are more likely to commit fully to thinking creatively.

In conclusion, encouraging innovative thinking is about more than just talking the talk. It's about creating a thriving environment, offering the right tools, fostering diverse perspectives, and leading by example. When you commit to these principles, you pave the way for a culture of innovation that can drive sustained organizational success.

Managing Creative Teams

Managing creative teams is both an art and a science. These teams bring unparalleled energy and vision, but they also pose unique challenges. Knowing how to balance creativity with structure is crucial for fostering innovation while maintaining productivity. First and foremost, it's important to create an environment where creativity can flourish.

Surrounding your team with the right resources can make a world of difference. Open spaces, plenty of natural light, and access to collaborative tools can stimulate fresh ideas and collaborative energy. However, it's not just about the physical environment. Encouraging a culture where experimentation and even failure are viewed as part of the creative process is essential. When people aren't afraid to fail, they're more likely to take risks and think outside the box.

Flexibility in how work gets done is another significant component. Creative endeavors often don't adhere to a nine-to-five schedule. Giving team members autonomy over their schedules can lead to heightened productivity and creativity. Maybe someone does their best brainstorming at midnight, or perhaps a walk in the park during the workday helps another develop a breakthrough idea.

But flexibility must be balanced with structure. Establishing clear, attainable goals can guide the creative process without stifling it. Providing deadlines can help keep the team on track, but those deadlines should be reasonable to avoid unnecessary pressure that can crush creativity. Consider implementing iterative processes, where the team can develop ideas over multiple stages—this allows for continuous improvement and refinement.

Leadership plays a critical role in managing creative teams. A good leader doesn't micromanage but instead provides support and empowers team members. Offering constructive feedback, celebrating small wins, and recognizing each individual's contribution can go a long way in maintaining morale and motivation. Authenticity and approachability from leaders can create a sense of trust and open dialogue.

Empathy is another cornerstone. Understanding the emotional landscape of a creative individual or team can help in mitigating stress and fostering a more harmonious environment. Stressful conditions can stifle creativity, so it's crucial to acknowledge and address any issues the team is facing. Sometimes, all it takes is a listening ear or a quick team-building exercise to reignite the creative spark.

A good leader knows how to facilitate collaboration and cross-pollination of ideas. Encouraging diverse viewpoints isn't just about having a mix of skills and backgrounds; it's about genuinely welcoming and integrating those diverse perspectives into the fabric of the project. Collaboration tools and techniques, such as brainstorming sessions, mind mapping, and regular check-ins, can ensure that everyone's voice is heard and valued.

Creating an environment of psychological safety is paramount. Team members should feel secure enough to share out-of-the-box ideas without the fear of ridicule or harsh criticism. When people feel safe, they're more willing to share novel concepts, challenge existing assumptions, and engage deeply in their work. Cultivating this type of environment often depends on setting the right tone from the top.

Innovation often springs from curiosity. Encourage questions and the relentless quest for improvement. Asking "Why?" and "What if?" might lead to the next big idea. A creative team thrives when curiosity is not just permitted but actively promoted. Integrate opportunities for learning and exploration into the team's routine.

Managing a creative team is also about managing energy. High levels of creativity can sometimes lead to burnout. It's important to keep an eye on the team's workload and offer breaks or changes of pace when necessary. Something as simple as a team outing or a creative workshop can recharge batteries and offer new sources of inspiration.

Measuring success with creative teams can be intricate. Traditional metrics might not capture the value a creative team brings. Instead, look at a combination of qualitative and quantitative measures. Project outcomes, team satisfaction, and even customer feedback can provide a fuller picture of a team's effectiveness. Sometimes, the true impact of creative work isn't evident until later, so patience and long-term thinking are beneficial.

Lastly, celebrating successes is vital. Creative endeavors can often be long and arduous journeys. Acknowledging and celebrating milestones along the way can keep the momentum going and let the team know that their work is valued. Whether it's through formal recognition, a team lunch, or even a simple "thank you" note, showing appreciation can have a big impact.

Effective leadership intertwines with empathy and a genuine care for your team's well-being. It's about creating a fertile ground where creativity can thrive. When done right, managing creative teams not only drives innovation but also builds a resilient, motivated, and high-performing unit.

Chapter 11:
Ethical Leadership

In today's complex and fast-paced world, ethical leadership is no longer a luxury—it's a necessity. It's about more than just following rules or keeping out of trouble; it's about embedding integrity into every fiber of an organization. Ethical leaders build trust and cultivate environments where people feel safe to be their authentic selves. They set the tone for what's acceptable, modeling behavior that aligns with the organization's core values. By holding themselves and others to high ethical standards, they not only foster workplace morale but also drive long-term success. Remember, leading ethically requires courage and a commitment to do what's right, even when it's hard. Balancing this with the pressures of the business world isn't always easy, but it's the foundation upon which lasting and meaningful leadership is built.

Defining Ethical Principles

Ethical principles serve as the cornerstone of effective leadership. They provide a guiding framework that informs decisions, shapes behaviors, and sets the tone for an organization's culture. Ethical leadership involves more than just adhering to laws and regulations; it's about cultivating a deeply-rooted sense of integrity and responsibility. By establishing clear ethical guidelines, leaders can create an environment where trust, respect, and fairness are paramount. But what exactly are these ethical principles, and how can they be defined in a way that resonates with employees at all levels? Let's dive in and explore.

First and foremost, transparency is a fundamental ethical principle. As a leader, being transparent means sharing information openly and honestly. It means admitting mistakes when they happen and being upfront about challenges the organization faces. Transparency fosters trust, and trust is the bedrock of any successful team. When employees feel they are in the loop, they're more likely to be engaged and committed. Transparency aligns with authenticity, avoiding any semblance of deception or half-truths.

Honesty and integrity go hand in hand with transparency, but they deserve their own spotlight. Integrity is the consistent practice of doing the right thing, even when no one is watching. It's the moral compass that guides a leader through complex and challenging situations. Honesty facilitates open communication and ensures that all stakeholders—employees, customers, and partners—are treated fairly. Leaders who embody integrity inspire their teams to act ethically, even in difficult circumstances.

Respect for others is another pivotal ethical principle. Respect involves recognizing the inherent worth of each team member and treating everyone with dignity. It encompasses valuing diverse perspectives and creating an inclusive environment where all voices are heard. Leaders who practice respect foster a positive and collaborative workplace culture, leading to higher morale and better overall performance.

Then there's accountability. It's crucial for leaders to be account-able both to themselves and to their teams. Accountability means owning up to one's actions, decisions, and their outcomes. A leader who is accountable demonstrates reliability and integrity. This principle encourages a culture of responsibility where everyone feels obligated to meet their commitments and contribute to the organization's success. When accountability is prioritized, it sets a standard for other team members to follow.

Fairness is another cornerstone principle in ethical leadership. Fair leaders make decisions impartially and ensure that resources and opportunities are distributed equitably. They avoid favoritism and bias, and instead, make choices that benefit the organization as a whole. Fairness leads to a sense of justice within the team and can significantly enhance employee satisfaction and loyalty. Everyone wants to feel they are being treated fairly—it's a simple yet powerful principle.

Additionally, consider the virtue of empathy. Empathy is the ability to understand and share the feelings of others. By practicing empathy, leaders can better connect with their team members on a personal level, addressing concerns and challenges with sensitivity and care. Empathy builds stronger interpersonal relationships and makes employees feel valued and understood. It's an essential element in effective leadership and helps create a supportive and nurturing work environment.

Leaders should also embrace the principle of ethical stewardship. This involves the responsible management of the organization's resources—including human, financial, and environmental resources—for the long-term benefit of all stakeholders. Ethical stewardship isn't just about ensuring profitability; it's about balancing the needs of shareholders with those of employees, the community, and the environment. It's a commitment to sustainability and ethical conduct in all business practices.

One often-overlooked ethical principle is courage. Leading with courage means taking bold actions that reflect your ethical values, even when those actions are not popular or easy. It involves standing up for what is right, confronting unethical behavior, and making decisions that align with your moral convictions. Courageous leaders set a powerful example and inspire their teams to act with integrity and determination.

Finally, humility is a critical ethical principle. Humble leaders recognize their limitations and are open to feedback and continuous learning. They don't see themselves as infallible and are willing to admit when they're wrong. Humility fosters a culture of collaboration and mutual respect, where everyone feels comfortable contributing their ideas and expertise. It's a reminder that leadership is not about personal glory but about serving the team and the greater good.

Defining ethical principles also involves articulating these values clearly and consistently. Leaders should outline their ethical principles in a code of conduct or ethical guidelines document, ensuring it is accessible to all team members. This codification helps prevent ambiguities and provides a reference point for decision-making. It's not enough to define ethical principles; they must be actively communicated, reinforced, and integrated into the daily operations of the organization.

Implementing ethical principles requires more than just documentation—it takes active effort and vigilance. Holding regular training sessions that focus on ethical behavior and decision-making can help embed these principles into the organizational culture. Encouraging open dialogue about ethics and providing channels for confidential reporting of unethical behavior are also crucial steps in maintaining an ethical workplace.

As you cultivate these ethical principles within your leadership style, remember that it's a journey, not a destination. Ethical leadership is an ongoing process that requires continuous reflection and adaptation. By setting high ethical standards and living by them, you can inspire your team to do the same, creating a ripple effect that positively impacts your organization and beyond.

In summary, ethical principles such as transparency, honesty, integrity, respect, accountability, fairness, empathy, ethical steward-ship, courage, and humility are the guiding beacons for effective leadership. By defining and embodying these principles, leaders can create a trustworthy, respectful, and high-performing workplace. Living these values out loud not only drives organizational success but also contributes to a more ethical and just world.

Maintaining Integrity and Trust

In your journey towards ethical leadership, maintaining integrity and trust isn't just a task—it's the cornerstone of your leadership philosophy. Without it, everything else falls apart. Trust is the glue that binds an organization together, and integrity is the magnet that keeps individuals aligned with a common purpose.

Let's start by defining what we mean by integrity. Integrity represents a steadfast adherence to a strict moral or ethical code. It's about being honest and having strong moral principles, even when it's inconvenient. Trust, on the other hand, is a belief in the reliability, truth, or ability of someone or something. When your team has trust in you and knows that you embody integrity, they're more likely to stay committed to your vision and perform at their best.

It's essential to understand that integrity in leadership is not a one-time act but a continuous practice. It's demonstrated through consistent actions and decisions that reflect your core values. When leaders act with integrity, they set the standard for their team, creating a culture where ethical behavior is the norm rather than the exception.

Consider the everyday decisions you make. Each choice is an opportunity to reinforce or erode trust. Are you transparent with your team about the challenges the organization faces? Do you follow through on your promises? Do you admit your mistakes and take responsibility? Answering 'yes' to these questions is a good indicator that you're on the right track.

Building and maintaining trust requires a commitment to authenticity and vulnerability. This might seem counterintuitive in a professional setting, but showing your human side can significantly impact how your team perceives you. Sharing your own challenges and failures not only makes you relatable but also fosters a more open and trusting environment where team members feel safe to share their own ideas and concerns.

Over time, the small, unassuming actions that demonstrate your commitment to integrity add up. They create a reservoir of trust that you can draw upon in times of crisis. Stephen Covey refers to this as the "emotional bank account," where every action you take either deposits or withdraws from the emotional reserves of your team. Maintaining a positive balance in this account is crucial for long-term leadership success.

Moreover, integrity and trust are particularly vital when faced with difficult decisions that might not be popular. Leaders often find themselves at a crossroads where upholding these values seems to conflict with short-term gains. It's in these moments that your integrity is genuinely tested. Choosing to do what's right, even when it's hard or unpopular, strengthens the trust your team has in you.

Openness and transparency are practical facets of maintaining integrity and trust. Being forthright about potential setbacks or the direction of the company prevents the spread of misinformation and builds a culture of honesty. When people are well-informed, they're more likely to trust the process and support the vision, even if they have reservations.

Regular communication plays a key role in ensuring that your team feels connected and trusted. Consistent updates, team meetings, and one-on-one check-ins offer opportunities to reinforce your commitment to integrity. These interactions should be honest and authentic, providing not just updates but a venue for open dialogue and feedback. Listening actively and responding thoughtfully to your team builds trust by showing that you value their input and are genuinely interested in their well-being.

Empathy is another fundamental aspect of building trust. Leaders who show genuine care for their team's personal and professional lives foster loyalty and trust. Understanding their challenges, celebrating their successes, and supporting their development are powerful ways to build a solid foundation of trust. When people feel valued and understood, they're more likely to resonate with your leadership and align their efforts with the organization's goals.

Accountability ties directly into maintaining integrity. Holding yourself and your team accountable ensures that everyone remains aligned with the organization's values and objectives. This isn't just about pointing fingers when things go wrong, but fostering a culture where everyone feels responsible and committed to upholding high standards. When team members see that accountability is a shared value, they trust that the team's success is a collective effort.

Inclusivity also plays a crucial role in establishing a culture of integrity and trust. Encouraging diverse perspectives and ensuring that everyone feels heard and respected strengthens the trust that individuals have in the leadership. Making decisions that consider the diverse views within your team builds an inclusive environment where integrity is a collective, shared principle.

Finally, fostering an environment where ethical behavior is rewarded rather than just expected can encourage the entire team to uphold these values. Recognizing and celebrating team members who exemplify integrity and trust reinforces these behaviors and sends a clear message about what the organization values. When people see that integrity is not just preached but practiced and celebrated, they're more likely to adopt these values themselves.

Trust takes years to build, seconds to break, and forever to repair. This saying highlights the fragility and importance of trust in leadership. Maintaining integrity and trust is a long-term investment that pays significant dividends in team cohesion, efficiency, and morale. It requires self-awareness, consistent actions, and a genuine commitment to ethical leadership principles.

In conclusion, maintaining integrity and trust is not an optional add-on for leaders; it's an essential part of effective and ethical leadership. It's about leading by example, being authentic, and making tough decisions that align with your values. By doing so, you not only build a high-performing team but also create a legacy of leadership that others will respect and strive to emulate.

Chapter 12:
Measuring Leadership Success

Measuring leadership success isn't just about hitting sales targets or driving growth—it's a holistic examination of the impact you have on your team, your organization, and even yourself. While Key Performance Indicators (KPIs) provide tangible metrics, the real magic happens when we marry these figures with a genuine commitment to continuous improvement. It's about celebrating wins but also digging deep into areas needing growth. Strong leaders know success is as much about fostering a positive culture and driving sustainable change as it is about meeting quarterly objectives. By adopting a multifaceted approach to evaluation, considering both the quantifiable and the qualitative, you can craft a leadership legacy that stands the test of time. Genuinely successful leadership ensures that your people are empowered, your strategies are agile, and your ethos remains unshakeable.

Key Performance Indicators (KPIs)

Measuring leadership success can be a complex endeavor. It's not just about meeting sales targets or reducing overhead costs; true leadership encompasses a blend of tangible and intangible elements. To effectively gauge this multifaceted role, Key Performance Indicators (KPIs) serve as a vital tool. KPIs offer a quantifiable measure that links leadership efforts directly to organizational outcomes. Setting the right

KPIs allows leaders to track performance, make informed decisions, and adjust strategies proactively.

KPIs are not just numbers on a dashboard; they're lifelines that connect the aspirations of a leader with the day-to-day realities of the organization. Think of them as the pulse points of your leadership journey. When chosen and monitored correctly, KPIs provide immediate feedback on whether you're moving towards your goals or veering off course. However, defining relevant KPIs requires careful consideration of the unique vision, mission, and strategic objectives of your organization.

It's essential to craft KPIs that align with both short-term activities and long-term goals. For instance, short-term KPIs might focus on quarterly revenue growth, while long-term KPIs could aim at enhancing customer satisfaction over the coming years. Effective KPIs should offer a balanced perspective, harmonizing immediate needs with enduring aspirations. This dual focus ensures adaptability in a constantly evolving business environment.

To begin, ensure your KPIs adhere to the SMART criteria— Specific, Measurable, Achievable, Relevant, and Time-bound. This framework simplifies the goal-setting process, making it less daunting to translate broad vision statements into actionable steps. For example, 'Increase team productivity' can evolve into a more tangible KPI such as 'Enhance team productivity by 15% within the next quarter by implementing new project management software.' This SMART KPI provides clarity and direction.

Once your KPIs are set, the next step is to communicate them effectively across your team and organization. Communication is key here; it's not simply about disseminating information but fostering a shared understanding of what these KPIs mean and why they matter. When your team understands the purpose behind these metrics, they are more likely to be engaged and aligned with your leadership goals.

Utilize various communication channels—meetings, dashboards, and even informal conversations to keep the objectives front and center.

Moreover, KPIs should not remain static. Regular reviews and adjustments are crucial to ensure they remain aligned with the evolving business landscape and organizational priorities. Create a habit of periodic KPI assessments, integrating feedback from your team and stakeholders. This open-loop system not only enhances the relevance of your KPIs but also fosters a culture of continuous improvement and adaptability.

Encourage ownership and accountability within your team concerning KPIs. When team members feel responsible for achieving these metrics, their engagement and commitment naturally increase. Foster an environment where KPIs are viewed as collective goals rather than individual pressures. Collaborative efforts can transform KPI targets into shared victories, enhancing team cohesion and overall morale.

Additionally, embedding a mix of leading and lagging indicators in your KPI framework can provide a more robust and predictive viewpoint. Leading indicators, such as the number of new customer inquiries, offer foresight and enable proactive leadership strategies. In contrast, lagging indicators like annual revenue provide insights into historical performance, allowing for reflective improvements. This balanced KPI approach ensures a comprehensive performance overview, mitigating risks, and capitalizing on opportunities effectively.

Also, consider the qualitative aspects of leadership success when defining KPIs. While quantitative metrics are crucial, they don't capture the entire picture. Incorporate qualitative KPIs like employee satisfaction scores and 360-degree feedback results to gauge the softer aspects of leadership, such as emotional intelligence and team dynamics. Sometimes, the impact of a leader's empathy or vision can't be distilled into numbers, and these qualitative indicators provide the nuanced understanding required.

Learning from past KPI performance is invaluable. Conducting post-mortem analyses on both successful and underwhelming KPIs can offer insights into what works and why. These reflections help fine-tune future KPI settings and foster a learning atmosphere that promotes growth and innovation. Don't shy away from failures; instead, treat them as rich learning experiences that contribute to personal and organizational development.

Technology can significantly enhance the effectiveness of KPIs. Leveraging advanced data analytics tools and KPI dashboards can provide real-time insights and predictive analytics, enabling more informed and timely decision-making. These digital tools can help visualize complex data, making it easier to communicate KPI progress across your team and stakeholders. Integrating technological solutions ensures that your KPIs are not only visible but also actionable.

It's equally important to celebrate KPI milestones and successes. Recognizing achievements, both big and small, can boost motivation and morale. When your team hits a KPI, take the time to acknowledge and celebrate this success. This acknowledgment can be a simple email shout-out, a team luncheon, or even a small rewards program. Celebrations reinforce positive behavior and set a precedent for future efforts.

Lastly, KPIs should serve as a guide, not a constriction. While it's essential to meet targets, flexibility and adaptability should be embedded within your KPI management approach. Organizational dynamics can change rapidly, and rigid adherence to outdated KPIs can stifle innovation and responsiveness. Be prepared to pivot and adjust your KPIs in response to new challenges and opportunities. This agile approach ensures that your leadership remains relevant and effective in a dynamically changing environment.

In conclusion, KPIs are not merely metrics but powerful tools that translate visionary leadership into tangible achievements. They provide a bridge between theoretical goals and actionable results, enabling leaders to steer their organizations towards success. Careful consideration, continuous improvement, and effective communication are the pillars of a robust KPI framework. Embrace the journey of setting, monitoring, and evolving your KPIs as a cornerstone of your leadership strategy. Remember, the ultimate objective is to foster a culture of continuous improvement, engagement, and achievement that drives your organization forward.

Continuous Improvement

As we bring our focus to measuring leadership success, it's essential to recognize the role of continuous improvement. The landscape of leadership isn't static; it's an ever-evolving journey marked by both achievements and lessons learned. Continuous improvement serves as the engine that propels leaders and their organizations forward, ensuring that successes are not just one-time events but the foundation for ongoing progress.

Leaders can't afford to rest on their laurels. The business world moves quickly, and those who fail to adapt are left behind. Continuous improvement is not merely a buzzword but a critical mindset for achieving sustainable growth and long-term success. It requires an ongoing commitment to evaluation, reflection, and action. This mindset pushes leaders to identify areas for enhancement, implement changes, and measure the impact of those changes.

One might ask, "How can leaders consistently improve?" The answer lies in fostering a culture that encourages feedback, supports experimentation, and rewards learning. By creating an environment where team members feel safe to voice their ideas and concerns, leaders can uncover valuable insights that might otherwise go unnoticed. This culture of openness and transparency is the bedrock of continuous improvement.

Feedback is the lifeblood of continuous improvement. It provides the essential data required to understand what's working and what's not. Effective leaders actively seek out feedback from all levels of the organization, as well as from external stakeholders such as customers and partners. But feedback alone isn't enough. The critical step is transforming this information into actionable strategies and interventions.

For instance, regular performance reviews and team meetings can serve as platforms for gathering feedback. These sessions shouldn't be seen merely as routine administrative tasks but as opportunities for growth and improvement. It's vital that leaders not only listen but also act on the feedback received. Implementing meaningful changes based on actionable insights demonstrates to the team that their input is valued and makes a difference.

It's also important to instill a mindset of experimentation. Encouraging a "fail-forward" attitude allows teams to test new ideas without the fear of repercussions. Not every experiment will succeed, and that's okay. Each failure is a learning opportunity, providing insights that can lead to innovation and improvement. Leaders who embrace this mindset foster a culture of creativity and resilience within their organizations.

Imagine a leadership team that treats each project as an experiment. They set clear objectives, measure results meticulously, and aren't afraid to pivot when things don't go as planned. This approach not only keeps the team agile and responsive but also relentlessly focused on bettering their strategies and processes.

Metrics play a crucial role in the process of continuous improvement. They offer a tangible way to track progress and measure the effectiveness of changes made. Key Performance Indicators (KPIs) should be closely monitored, but they should also be flexible enough to evolve as the organization grows. Sometimes, the metrics that served well in the past may no longer be relevant or sufficient for driving future success.

To keep metrics relevant, leaders need to periodically reassess their KPIs in alignment with evolving business goals and market conditions. This is not a set-it-and-forget-it exercise; it demands ongoing diligence and adjustment. Leaders should be prepared to refine KPIs to ensure they continue to provide meaningful insights that guide decision-making and improvement efforts.

Moreover, leaders must champion the philosophy of "kaizen," a Japanese term meaning "change for better." This philosophy promotes continuous, incremental improvements in all aspects of life. When applied in a business context, kaizen embodies a systematic approach to identify inefficiencies and introduce refinements. It involves everyone in the organization, from top executives to frontline employees, fostering a collective responsibility for improvement.

Consider the story of a company that implemented kaizen across its operations. The leadership team encouraged every employee to suggest daily improvements, no matter how small. Over time, these incremental changes added up to significant enhancements in efficiency, quality, and employee morale. This is the power of continuous improvement in action.

Encouraging lifelong learning is another pillar of continuous improvement. Leaders who invest in their own development set a powerful example for their teams. Whether through formal education, professional workshops, or self-study, the commitment to learning keeps leaders sharp and adaptable in a rapidly changing world. Additionally, fostering a culture where ongoing education is valued ensures that the entire organization remains competitive.

Equally important is the notion of reflective practice. Leaders must regularly take the time to reflect on their experiences, decisions, and their overall leadership journey. Reflection provides the clarity needed to understand past actions, recognize patterns, and plan more effectively for the future. By dedicating time to self-reflection, leaders gain insight into their strengths and areas for improvement, enabling them to lead with greater self-awareness and purpose.

Leadership success isn't a destination but a continuous journey governed by a commitment to constant learning and adaptation. Continuous improvement is the compass that helps leaders navigate this journey, driving them and their organizations toward ever-higher levels of performance and achievement. As we explore different dimensions of leadership, it's crucial to remember that the quest for improvement never truly ends. It is an enduring process that turns ordinary experiences into extraordinary lessons, and these lessons into the stepping stones of lasting success.

Conclusion

As we bring this exploration of leadership to a close, it's essential to reflect on the journey we've taken and the insights gained. Leadership isn't merely about holding a title or managing tasks; it's a continuous evolution, a dynamic interplay of skills, attitudes, and behaviors that collectively inspire and drive an organization towards success. The path to effective leadership is neither linear nor easy, but it's undoubtedly rewarding.

Throughout this book, we've ventured through the intricacies of the leadership mindset, the importance of vision, and the necessity of strategic planning. These foundational elements serve as the bedrock upon which effective leadership is built. A leader's mindset isn't just a mental state; it's an ongoing commitment to growth, empathy, and resilience. By fostering a mindset geared towards excellence and continuous improvement, leaders can inspire their teams to reach new heights.

Crafting and communicating a clear vision is pivotal. A vision isn't just a sweeping statement of future aspirations; it encapsulates the dreams and direction of the organization. It serves as a beacon, guiding decisions and actions, and providing a sense of purpose and motivation for every team member. A well-communicated vision establishes a shared understanding that aligns everyone towards common goals, fostering unity and collaborative effort.

Strategic planning transforms vision into actionable steps. By setting clear goals and priorities, and ensuring alignment with the overall vision, leaders can create robust strategies that propel the organization forward. Effective leaders are not just dreamers but doers. They take the aspirations encapsulated in their vision and translate them into a strategic roadmap filled with achievable milestones.

Building effective teams is perhaps one of the most challenging yet rewarding aspects of leadership. Great leaders recognize the power of a cohesive, motivated team. They invest time in recruiting the right talent, nurturing their growth, and fostering an environment where collaboration flourishes. A team that feels valued and understood will go above and beyond to achieve collective goals.

Change is the only constant, and leading through change is a critical skill for any leader. Organizations face ever-evolving challenges, and leaders must be adept at navigating these waters. Developing resilience in oneself and one's team ensures that changes – whether anticipated or abrupt – are met with agility and grace. Resilience is not about avoiding difficulties but about facing them head-on and emerging stronger.

Decision-making, while often daunting, is an integral part of leadership. The ability to balance analytical assessment with intuitive judgment sets great leaders apart. Employing diverse decision-making frameworks can provide leaders with the tools they need to navigate complex challenges and seize opportunities effectively. Good decision-making is underpinned by thorough analysis and an intuitive understanding of the human elements involved.

Emotional intelligence is the thread that weaves through every aspect of effective leadership. Leaders who are self-aware, who understand and manage their emotions, and who demonstrate empathy and robust social skills, are those who can forge strong relationships and inspire unwavering loyalty. Emotional intelligence enables leaders to connect with their teams on a human level, creating an atmosphere of trust and mutual respect.

Communication skills are indispensable. Whether it's through inspiring public speaking or through active listening and constructive feedback, effective communication binds a leader to their team. It's through communication that visions are shared, goals are set, and feedback is given and received. Mastering the art of communication ensures that messages are not only heard but understood and embraced.

Conflict resolution is another critical competency. Conflicts are inevitable in any dynamic environment, and the ability to identify sources of conflict and manage them constructively can make or break a team's cohesion and productivity. Leaders who handle conflicts with aplomb foster an environment where challenges can be addressed openly and solutions can be reached collaboratively.

Innovation and creativity are the lifeblood of progressive organizations. Leaders who champion innovative thinking and skillfully manage creative teams drive their organizations towards unprecedented success. Encouraging a culture that values creativity ensures that new ideas thrive and that the organization remains competitive in an ever-evolving market.

Ethical leadership is not just about adhering to rules but about embodying principles of integrity, honesty, and fairness. In a world where trust is easily eroded, maintaining ethical standards is paramount. Leaders who prioritize ethics and build a culture of trust and integrity set their organizations apart and inspire loyalty and respect from both within and outside their teams.

Measuring leadership success is not a one-time effort but an ongoing process. Utilizing key performance indicators (KPIs) provides objective measures of progress and areas for improvement. Continuous improvement is the hallmark of a proactive leader who is always looking for ways to enhance their effectiveness and that of their team.

In closing, the accumulation of these competencies and the continuous application of these principles form the essence of extraordinary leadership. As you continue your journey, remember that leadership is an ever-evolving practice. It's about striving not for perfection but for progress, fostering a culture of learning, and embracing each challenge as an opportunity to grow.

Empower yourself and your team. Lead with empathy and vision. Plan strategically, communicate effectively, and navigate changes with resilience. Make decisions judiciously, foster innovation, uphold ethical standards, and strive for continuous improvement. By embodying these qualities, you will not only achieve organizational success but also leave a lasting legacy that inspires those who follow in your footsteps.

Remember, the true measure of leadership lies in the impact you have on others – inspiring them to dream more, learn more, do more, and become more.

Appendix A:
Appendix

In our journey through the realms of leadership, we've encountered numerous insights and actionable strategies designed to empower you to lead with purpose and impact. This appendix serves as an essential companion to the core content of the book, providing you with practical tools and additional resources to further develop your leadership skills.

Practical Exercises and Worksheets

The following exercises are crafted to help you apply the concepts explored throughout this book. By engaging with these activities, you're not just learning; you're actively transforming theoretical knowledge into practical skills that will benefit you and your organization.

Leadership Self-Assessment: Reflect on your leadership style, strengths, and areas for improvement. This exercise will help you establish a baseline from which to grow.

Vision Crafting Workshop: Follow the steps outlined to articulate a compelling vision for your team or organization. Use the worksheet to draft, refine, and communicate your vision effectively.

Strategic Planning Template: Utilize this template to set clear goals, priorities, and actionable strategies that align with your vision.

Team Building Activities: Engage in exercises designed to foster collaboration, trust, and high performance within your team.

Change Management Plan: Develop a detailed plan to navigate and lead through organizational change, focusing on resilience and adaptability.

Decision-Making Framework: Apply analytical and intuitive approaches to decision-making scenarios presented in the worksheet, helping you hone your judgment.

Emotional Intelligence Journal: Use daily prompts to enhance your self-awareness, self-regulation, empathy, and social skills.

Communication Practice Sessions: Engage in structured practice sessions to improve your public speaking and active listening skills.

Conflict Resolution Scenarios: Work through real-world conflict scenarios using the strategies discussed, aiming for constructive outcomes.

Innovation Challenge: Encourage innovative thinking within your team by setting up challenges that stimulate creativity and problem-solving.

Ethical Dilemmas: Analyze and resolve ethical dilemmas using the principles covered in the book, reinforcing your commitment to integrity and trust.

Leadership KPI Tracker: Track your progress using key performance indicators, and identify opportunities for continuous improvement using the provided tracker.

Additional Resources

To supplement your growth, we've compiled a list of additional resources that can further deepen your understanding and expand your leadership toolkit:

Books: Explore a curated list of influential books on leadership, psychology, emotional intelligence, and strategic planning.

Podcasts: Listen to thought-provoking interviews and discussions with industry leaders and experts.

Online Courses: Enroll in recommended online courses that offer comprehensive modules on various aspects of leadership.

Webinars and Workshops: Participate in live and recorded sessions that provide interactive learning experiences and networking opportunities.

Tools and Software: Discover digital tools and software that can streamline your leadership activities, from goal setting to team collaboration and project management.

Remember, growth is an ongoing process. As you continue to evolve in your leadership journey, these exercises and resources will serve as valuable aids, guiding you toward becoming the leader you aspire to be. Stay committed, remain curious, and always strive for excellence.

Let's turn these insights into action and make a lasting impact on our teams, our organizations, and ourselves.

Practical Exercises and Worksheets

Developing leadership skills isn't just about understanding theories and concepts—it's about putting those principles into practice. The "Practical Exercises and Worksheets" section is designed to offer you hands-on opportunities to apply what you've learned. Here, you'll find a variety of exercises and worksheets tailored to enhance different aspects of your leadership capabilities. Whether you're a seasoned manager or an aspiring leader, these tools will serve as a roadmap for your development journey.

Let's start with *self-assessment exercises*. Understanding your current capabilities and areas for improvement is the first step towards growth. Self-assessment isn't just a self-reflection activity; it's an introspective journey. Set aside some quiet time to answer questions regarding your leadership style, emotional intelligence, and decision-making processes. Be brutally honest with yourself. Remember, growth begins where comfort zones end.

For example, you might use a **Self-Awareness Worksheet** that's divided into sections such as strengths, weaknesses, opportunities, and threats (SWOT analysis). By recognizing your SWOT, you're better positioned to leverage your strengths and improve your weaknesses. This exercise demands candidness and self-compassion. After completing this worksheet, review your responses. Are there surprises, or do the areas of improvement confirm what you already knew? Use these insights to set actionable goals for yourself.

Another invaluable tool in this section is the **Goal-Setting Exercise**. Many leaders falter because they don't have a clear path or don't stick to it. This exercise guides you in setting SMART (Specific, Measurable, Achievable, Relevant, Time-bound) goals. The worksheet prompts you to focus on short-term and long-term objectives. As you write down your goals, visualize the steps you need to take to achieve them. This isn't just a bureaucratic task; it's a transformative practice that can make your vision tangible.

Then, there's the *Team Dynamics Worksheet*. Building an effective team requires more than just hiring the right people; it necessitates understanding and fostering collaboration. This worksheet includes questions about team strengths, individual roles, and collective goals. You can use the results to craft better team strategies and enhance productivity. This worksheet encourages you to facilitate open dialogues among team members, fostering an environment where everyone feels heard and valued.

Next, let's talk about **Conflict Resolution Exercises**. Conflict is inevitable, but how you manage it can make or break your leadership. Engage with role-playing activities that mimic real-life scenarios. These exercises help you practice and refine your conflict-handling skills. By rehearsing these scenarios, you become better equipped to handle actual conflicts with grace and efficacy.

One particularly effective exercise is the **Reflective Practice Journal**. Keeping a journal where you jot down daily reflections about your leadership experiences is an excellent way to improve self-awareness and emotional intelligence. Use prompts to guide your entries, such as "Describe a leadership challenge you faced today. How did you handle it? What could you have done differently?" This diaristic approach doesn't just help you improve; it also serves as a record of your leadership journey, a tangible reminder of how far you've come.

Consider also the **Vision Crafting Worksheet**. This tool is designed to help you articulate a clear and compelling vision for your team or organization. Answer questions related to your mission, core values, and long-term objectives. Use a combination of charts and narrative sections to make your vision as vivid and relatable as possible. Remember, a well-defined vision isn't just a guiding star for your organization; it's a beacon that attracts and inspires others.

Another vital component is **Strategic Planning Exercises**. In this section, you'll find detailed templates for drafting strategic plans. These worksheets break down the process into manageable chunks, covering everything from initial brainstorming to final execution. Use these tools to align your strategy with your vision, setting milestones and benchmarks to measure progress. Applying a structured approach to strategic planning not only clarifies your path forward but also makes it easier to adjust and pivot as circumstances change.

The **Feedback Loop Worksheet** is another essential tool. Effective leaders constantly seek and provide feedback. This worksheet guides you through the process of establishing feedback loops within your team. It encourages transparency and fosters a culture of continuous improvement. By regularly soliciting feedback, you show your team that you value their input, which can significantly enhance morale and productivity.

Emotional intelligence (EI) is another cornerstone of effective leadership. To this end, you'll find the **EI Skills Assessment** particularly useful. This worksheet includes questions designed to measure your competency in various EI domains, such as self-awareness, self-regulation, motivation, empathy, and social skills. Understanding where you stand in these areas helps you focus your development efforts more precisely. Complement this with practical exercises to enhance each aspect of EI, such as active listening drills and empathy-building activities.

The *Decision-Making Frameworks Worksheet* will also help you refine your decision-making skills. This tool guides you through different frameworks, from analytical to intuitive approaches. By practicing decisions in hypothetical scenarios, you can better understand which framework plays to your strengths. This exercise aims to build your confidence in making sound decisions under pressure, a critical skill for any leader.

One more exercise you might find useful is the **Values Alignment Worksheet**. It's vital to ensure that your actions align with your values. This worksheet guides you in articulating your core values and evaluating how well your actions reflect them. By identifying any misalignments, you can take steps to better integrate your values into your daily leadership practices.

Finally, look into **Public Speaking Drills** included in this section. Great leaders are often great orators. These drills can help you improve your public speaking skills. Practice crafting persuasive messages, engage in mock presentations, and use the provided checklists to evaluate your performance. Confidence in public speaking can profoundly influence how you connect with your team and stakeholders.

The exercises and worksheets included in this section are more than just activities to fill your time—they are powerful tools designed to foster growth and development. They represent deliberate practice, a concept backed by research showing that expertise doesn't just come from experience but from mindful, purposeful practice. By actively engaging with these exercises, you're not just learning about leadership; you're becoming a leader. Equip yourself with these tools, and set forth on your journey of continuous improvement.

Additional Resources

For leaders committed to personal and organizational growth, there's a treasure trove of additional resources that can be a catalyst for success. It's crucial to never stop learning, and the resources found in this section will help guide that continuous journey. From insightful books and cutting-edge research to seminars and online courses, the following tools can help deepen your understanding and expand your leadership capabilities.

Books and Publications

Books are often the cornerstone of leadership development. Classics like "Good to Great" provide timeless principles that every leader can incorporate into their strategic thinking. Newer publications delve into the nuances of tech-driven leadership, adaptive strategies, and empathetic management styles. Top-rated business and leadership magazines, such as "Harvard Business Review" and "Forbes," offer frequent updates, thought-provoking articles, and case studies from industry front-runners.

Investing time in reading these invaluable texts can introduce new perspectives and reinforce fundamental concepts. They often include practical tips, real-world examples, and exercises that can help with day-to-day decision-making and long-term strategy formulation.

Professional Development Programs

Executive education programs are another potent resource, providing a deep dive into leadership skills through structured curriculums. Universities and business schools offer tailored courses that range from brief workshops to intensive months-long programs. These courses are often designed by industry veterans and academic experts, ensuring a rich, diverse learning experience.

Such programs are not just for acquiring knowledge; they also provide an invaluable opportunity to network with peers and mentors. Building relationships with other driven professionals can open doors to new opportunities and collaborative ventures.

Online Learning Platforms

In the digital age, the *accessibility* of quality education has been a game-changer. Online platforms like Coursera, LinkedIn Learning, and Udemy offer a multitude of courses on leadership, management strategies, and other relevant topics. These platforms often feature courses by world-renowned experts, providing insights that are both practical and cutting-edge.

The flexibility offered by these online courses is another significant advantage. Busy professionals can learn at their own pace, revisiting complex topics and fitting studies into their own schedules. Many of these courses also offer certifications that can be added to your professional portfolio, showcasing your commitment to ongoing improvement.

Conferences and Seminars

Attending industry conferences and seminars can also be wildly beneficial. These events often feature keynote speeches from successful leaders, panel discussions on critical industry trends, and interactive workshops. Moreover, they serve as a great platform for networking and sharing knowledge with peers.

Keep an eye out for local and international events focused on leadership or specific to your industry. Even in the realm of virtual conferences, the interaction and takeaways can be incredibly enriching.

Mentorship and Coaching

A mentor or a coach can provide personalized guidance that is hard to match through self-study. Engaging with someone who has 'been there, done that,' can provide invaluable insights and shortcuts to achieving your goals. Whether through formal programs or informal arrangements, having a mentor provides an opportunity for candid conversations, feedback, and advice tailored to your specific challenges.

Seeking out a coach can add another layer of targeted development. Coaching often focuses on harnessing existing strengths and navigating past limitations. It's a partnership where you set the agenda and the coach helps you to achieve it.

Peer Groups and Mastermind Groups

Joining a peer group or a mastermind group can also be incredibly impactful. These groups offer a safe space to discuss challenges, share successes, and gain different perspectives. Regular meetings with a group of peers can help in staying accountable and motivated.

Additionally, these groups often bring together professionals from diverse backgrounds and industries. This diversity can provide fresh insights and innovative solutions to common problems faced in leadership positions.

Research and Case Studies

Conducting research and reviewing case studies can provide concrete examples of how different leadership styles and strategies play out in the real world. Universities, business schools, and consulting firms frequently publish in-depth analyses of successful companies and leaders. These case studies can offer actionable insights that can be applied to your own organization's particular context.

Whether it's learning from the scalability strategies of tech giants or the customer-centric approaches of retail leaders, these case studies serve as valuable tools for contextual learning.

Journals and Articles

Academic journals and articles offer a more formalized and research-backed perspective on leadership theories and practices. Subscribing to key journals like the "Journal of Leadership Studies" or "The Leadership Quarterly" ensures you receive the latest developments and scholarly insights in the field.

These journals are filled with peer-reviewed articles that delve into various facets of leadership, from emotional intelligence to organizational behavior. Reading these works can help you stay abreast of academic advancements and emerging trends.

Podcasts and Webinars

In an age where multi-tasking is routine, podcasts and webinars present a convenient way to consume leadership content. There are countless podcasts hosted by influential leaders who share their stories, challenges, and advice. Similarly, webinars often feature experts who tackle specific issues, offering practical solutions and fostering interactive Q&A sessions.

These resources can be consumed during commutes, workouts, or even while taking a break from work, making it easy to integrate learning into your daily routine.

Every leadership journey is unique, and the best resources for one person might differ for another. The key is to remain curious and proactive in seeking out opportunities for growth and improvement. Embrace a mix of these resources to enrich your leadership toolkit, broaden your perspective, and empower yourself with the insights and skills needed to drive success.

www.ingramcontent.com/pod-product-compliance
Lightning Source LLC
Chambersburg PA
CBHW022018170526
45157CB00003B/1281